ASVAB
CORE REVIEW

2nd Edition

LEARNINGEXPRESS®

NEW YORK

Copyright © 2005 LearningExpress, LLC.

All rights reserved under International and Pan-American Copyright Conventions.
Published in the United States by LearningExpress, LLC, New York.

Library of Congress Cataloging-in-Publication Data:
ASVAB core review.—2nd ed.
   p. cm.
  ISBN 978-1-57685-479-2
  1. Armed Services Vocational Aptitude Battery—Study guides. I. Title: Armed services
vocational aptitude battery core review.
U408.5.A84 2005
355'.0076—dc22

                                               2004024724

Printed in the United States of America

9 8 7 6 5 4 3

Second Edition

Regarding the Information in this Book
We attempt to verify the information presented in our books prior to publication. It is always a good idea, however, to double-check such important information as minimum requirements, application and testing procedures, and deadlines with your local recruitment agency, as such information can change from time to time.

For information on LearningExpress, other LearningExpress products, or bulk sales, please write to us at:
   LearningExpress
   2 Rector Street
   26th Floor
   New York, NY 10006

Or visit us at:
   www.learnatest.com

Contents

List of Contributors

The following individuals contributed to the content of this book.

Elizabeth Chesla is the author of *501 Vocabulary Questions, TOEFL Exam Success, Reading Comprehension Success, Write Better Essays,* and contributing author of *GMAT Exam Success, ACT Exam Success, GED Exam Success,* and many other writing and reading guides and test-preparation books. She lives in Harleysville, Pennsylvania.

Mary Hesalroad, a former police officer for the Austin, Texas, Police Department, consults with police departments on recruiting efforts and is a freelance writer now living in Austin, Texas.

Judith N. Meyers is director of the Two Together Tutorial Program of the Jewish Child Care Association in New York City and an adult basic education practitioner.

Judith Robinovitz is an independent educational consultant and director of Score At the Top, a comprehensive test preparation program in Vero Beach, Florida.

Jo Lynn Southard is a freelance writer and editor living in Portland, Maine.

Shirley Tarbell is a test development specialist and writer living in Portland, Maine.

C H A P T E R

1 ▶ What Is the ASVAB Core?

CHAPTER SUMMARY

In order to enlist in the military, you have to take the Armed Services Vocational Aptitude Battery (ASVAB). But you only have to pass *four* of the eight subtests on the ASVAB to qualify for enlistment. This chapter explains those four subtests and shows you how to use this book to score your best.

The ASVAB is a multiple-aptitude test battery consisting of eight subtests. Four of these subtests—General Science, Auto and Shop Information, Mechanical Comprehension, and Electronics Information—are designed to determine what your aptitudes are for different jobs. However, only *four* of the ASVAB subtests—Arithmetic Reasoning, Word Knowledge, Paragraph Comprehension, and Mathematics Knowledge—count toward your Armed Forces Qualifying Test (AFQT) score, which determines whether or not you can enlist in the military. This book will cover only the four subtests that count toward your AFQT, referred to in this book as the *ASVAB core.*

NUMBER OF ITEMS AND TESTING TIME FOR THE ASVAB		
SUBTEST	NUMBER OF QUESTIONS	TIME (MINUTES)
General Science (GS)	25	11
Arithmetic Reasoning (AR)	**30**	**36**
Word Knowledge (WK)	**25**	**11**
Paragraph Comprehension (PC)	**15**	**13**
Auto and Shop Information (AS)	25	11
Mathematics Knowledge (MK)	**35**	**24**
Mechanical Comprehension (MC)	25	19
Electronics Information (EI)	20	9
Total	**200 items**	**134 minutes**

Note: Bolded items count toward the Armed Forces Qualifying Test (AFQT) score.

▶ The Four ASVAB Core Subtests

Following is a more detailed description of each of the four subtests that counts towards the AFQT score.

Part 1: Arithmetic Reasoning

The Arithmetic Reasoning subtest consists of 30 word problems describing everyday life situations, which are designed to measure your reasoning skills and understanding of:

- operations with whole numbers
- operations with fractions and decimals or money
- ratio and proportion
- interest and percentage
- measurement of perimeters, areas, volumes, and time and temperature

Chapter 6 will review math and Chapter 7 gives you extra practice in math.

Part 2: Word Knowledge

The Word Knowledge subtest consists of 25 questions that ask you to choose the correct definitions of verbs,

nouns, adjectives, and adverbs. These questions come in two forms:

- definitions presented alone, with no context
- words in the context of a short sentence

The vocabulary skills you need for the Word Knowledge subtest are presented in Chapter 8. Chapter 9 gives you more practice using these skills.

Part 3: Paragraph Comprehension

The Paragraph Comprehension subtest is 15 questions based on several short passages written on a variety of topics. No prior knowledge of the subject will be required—all the information you will need to answer the questions will be found in the passage. The questions test two different skills:

- **Literal comprehension:** your ability to identify stated facts, identify reworded facts, and determine the sequence of events
- **Implicit, inferential, or critical comprehension:** your ability to draw conclusions; identify the

main idea of a paragraph; determine the author's purpose, mood, or tone; and identify style and technique

Chapter 10 gives you the skills you need to do well on this subtest. Chapter 11 gives you more instruction on how to read well, and also gives you more practice reading questions.

Part 4: Mathematics Knowledge

The Mathematics Knowledge subtest consists of 35 questions designed to measure your understanding of mathematical concepts, principles, and procedures. The emphasis is on your ability to recognize and apply basic mathematical principles. The questions cover:

- **Number theory:** factors, multiples, reciprocals, number properties, primes, integers
- **Numeration:** fractional parts, decimals, percentages, and conversions; order of operations; exponents; rounding; reducing fractions; roots and radicals; signed numbers
- **Algebraic operations and equations:** solving or determining equations, factoring, simplifying algebraic expressions, converting a sentence to an equation
- **Geometry and measurement:** coordinates and slope, Pythagorean theorem, angle measurement, properties of polygons and circles, perimeter, area, volume, unit conversion
- **Probability:** determining the likelihood of an event occurring or not

These mathematical concepts are covered in Chapter 6 of this book, and Chapter 7 presents more problems for extra practice.

▶ Arranging to Take the ASVAB

If you are in high school, ask your guidance counselor about taking the ASVAB. Many high schools offer the ASVAB at a specific time during the school year.

If you are on your own, go to the nearest recruiter of the branch of the armed services you're interested in. There is no charge to take the ASVAB. Taking the exam does not obligate you to join the military, although you can probably expect to receive more detailed information about the many job opportunities available through the Army, Air Force, Navy, Marine Corps, and Coast Guard.

▶ What the ASVAB Means for You

If you want to enter the military, everything is riding on your ASVAB score. Your scores on the four subtests of the ASVAB covered in this book—the AFQT—determine whether you can get in at all. Once you are in, scores on the other subtests determine for which jobs, or Military Occupational Specialties, you will be allowed to train. For instance, if you want to learn to be a computer operator, you need good scores in Paragraph Comprehension, Word Knowledge, Mathematics Knowledge, General Science, and Mechanical Comprehension. But if you don't meet a certain minimum score in Paragraph Comprehension, Word Knowledge, Arithmetic Reasoning, and Mathematics Knowledge, you won't even be able to enlist.

If you are looking toward a career in the armed forces, you need to score well on the ASVAB. Fortunately, this book is here to help.

► How to Use This Book to Increase Your Score

The key to success in almost any field is to prepare for all you're worth. One of the very best ways to prepare for the ASVAB is to read and study this book, take the practice tests, and measure how you are progressing.

To ensure you are clear on the basic information, start by reading Chapter 2, which explains the recruitment and enlistment process, and how the ASVAB fits into that process. To learn more about the score you need to enlist, read Chapter 3 next.

Next, Chapter 4 takes you through the Learning-Express Test Preparation System. The nine steps in this chapter will ensure you are in top physical and mental shape to do your best on test day.

Armed with the knowledge you have gained in the first four chapters, take the first of three practice tests in Chapter 5. By taking this test, you will be able to see how you would perform if it were test day. Based on your score, you can also recognize your strengths and weaknesses and tailor the rest of your preparation before the actual test. Chapters 6 through 11 include targeted review and practice for each of the four subtests that count toward the all-important AFQT score.

Finally, Chapters 12 and 13 include two additional practice tests. Use these two tests to track your progress since the first test. You can return to the review and practice chapters as needed to ensure that you are focusing on the material that you find the most difficult.

Practice and preparation are the keys to doing well on this or any exam. This book will give you everything you need to score your best. Good luck!

Getting into the Military

CHAPTER SUMMARY

You may find joining the military an appealing career choice. Once you have made the decision that the military is where you are headed, you will need to be armed with information about the enlistment process. That is what this chapter has to offer.

Your introduction to the enlistment process usually starts with a visit to your local recruiting office. A look in the yellow pages of your phone book under "Recruiting" should give you the phone numbers and addresses of the nearest offices, or you can look in the blue government pages for one of the specific branches, if you have already decided on one.

Don't narrow your options too soon, though. If you are thinking of a career in the military, try visiting a recruiter from each of the five branches—Army, Navy, Air Force, Marines, and Coast Guard. There are lots of similarities, but the subtle differences in what each branch of service has to offer you could make a lot of difference in your career.

Throughout the enlistment process, you will have to present certain documents. Have the following available to ensure you are prepared:

- birth certificate or other proof of citizenship and date of birth
- valid Social Security card or two other pieces of Social Security identification
- high school diploma or GED certificate
- letter or transcript documenting your midterm graduation from high school, if applicable
- college transcript, if applicable, showing credits earned
- parental or guardian consent form if you are under 18 years old
- doctor's letter if you have, or have a history of, special medical condition(s)
- marriage certificate, if applicable
- divorce papers, if applicable

► Basic Requirements

There are certain requirements you will have to meet in order to enlist in any branch of the military. You must:

- be between 17 and 34 years of age, or have a parent or guardian's permission if you are under 18
- have a high school diploma or GED
- be drug-free
- have a clean arrest record

It is important to be truthful with your recruiter about any trouble you have had in the past with drugs or with the law. Criminal history checks are conducted on applicants. However, some kinds of problems can be overcome, if they are really *in the past,* not current difficulties. Check with your recruiter.

► Working with Your Recruiter

The recruiter is there to help you. In speaking with him or her, you will have the opportunity to ask as many questions as you want and to get a detailed picture of what each branch has to offer if you shop around. All recruiters will have brochures, videotapes, pamphlets, and years of personal experience to offer as resources. Don't be afraid to bring along a parent or a trusted friend to help you ask questions. A professional military recruiter won't mind the extra set of eyes and ears.

You can ask about the service and its benefits—salaries and fringe benefits, postings, and educational opportunities, including financial aid for college once you get out. (See the table on page 7 for the basic salary for various grades of enlisted personnel in all the services.) The recruiter will also ask about you: your education, your physical and mental health, and all sorts of in-depth questions about your goals, interests, hobbies, and life experience.

Before you take the Armed Services Vocational Aptitude Battery (ASVAB), you will be given a brief test designed to give the recruiter an idea of how well you will perform on the real test. This pretest covers math and vocabulary. Although the ASVAB has eight different subtests, it's the math and verbal portions that determine whether or not you pass the test. The other sections are designed to discover what your aptitudes are for different jobs. There is no limit to how many times you can take this brief test in the recruiter's office.

Your recruiter will talk to you about the benefits of enlisting: the pay, the travel, the experience, and the training. You and your recruiter can also start to discuss the kinds of jobs available to you in the military. But

The 2005 Military Pay Chart

Grade	<2	2	3	4	6	8	10	12	14	16	18	20	22	24	26
Commissioned Officers															
O-10	$0.00	$0.00	$0.00	$0.00	$0.00	$0.00	$0.00	$0.00	$0.00	$0.00	$0.00	$12963.00	$13026.60	$13297.50	$13769.40
O-9	0.00	0.00	0.00	0.00	0.00	0.00	0.00	0.00	0.00	0.00	0.00	11337.90	11501.10	11737.20	12149.10
O-8	8022.30	8285.10	8459.40	8508.30	8725.50	9089.40	9173.70	9519.00	9618.00	9915.30	10345.50	10742.40	11007.60	11007.60	11007.60
O-7	6666.00	6975.60	7119.00	7233.00	7439.10	7642.50	7878.30	8113.50	8349.00	9089.40	9714.60	9714.60	9714.60	9714.60	9763.80
O-6	4940.70	5427.90	5784.00	5784.00	5805.90	6054.90	6087.00	6087.90	6433.80	7045.50	7404.60	7763.40	7967.70	8174.10	8575.50
O-5	4118.70	4639.80	4961.10	5021.40	5221.50	5341.80	5605.50	5799.00	6048.60	6431.10	6613.20	6793.20	6997.50	6997.50	6997.50
O-4	3553.80	4113.90	4388.40	4449.60	4704.30	4977.60	5317.50	5582.70	5766.60	5872.20	5933.70	5933.70	5933.70	5933.70	5933.70
O-3	3124.50	3542.10	3823.20	4168.20	4367.70	4586.70	4728.60	4962.00	5083.20	5083.20	5083.20	5083.20	5083.20	5083.20	5083.20
O-2	2699.40	3074.70	3541.20	3660.90	3736.20	3736.20	3736.20	3736.20	3736.20	3736.20	3736.20	3736.20	3736.20	3736.20	3736.20
O-1	2343.60	2439.00	2948.10	2948.10	2948.10	2948.10	2948.10	2948.10	2948.10	2948.10	2948.10	2948.10	2948.10	2948.10	2948.10
Commissioned Officers with over 4 years active duty service as an enlisted member or warrant officer															
O-3E				4168.20	4367.70	4586.70	4728.60	4962.00	5158.50	5271.00	5424.60	5424.60			
O-2E				3660.90	3736.20	3855.30	4055.70	4211.10	4326.60	4326.60	4326.60	4326.60			
O-1E				2948.10	3148.80	3264.90	3383.70	3500.70	3660.90	3660.90	3660.90	3660.90			
Warrant Officers															
W-5	$0.00	$0.00	$0.00	$0.00	$0.00	$0.00	$0.00	$0.00	$0.00	$0.00	$0.00	$5548.20	$5738.40	$5929.20	$6121.20
W-4	3228.60	3473.40	3573.30	3671.40	3840.30	4007.10	4176.30	4341.00	4511.70	4779.00	4950.00	5117.40	5290.80	5461.80	5636.40
W-3	2948.40	3071.70	3197.40	3238.80	3371.10	3522.30	3721.80	3918.90	4128.30	4285.50	4442.10	4509.30	4578.90	4730.10	4881.30
W-2	2593.50	2741.70	2871.30	2965.50	3046.20	3268.20	3438.00	3564.00	3687.00	3771.30	3842.40	3977.40	4111.50	4247.40	4247.40
W-1	2290.20	2477.70	2603.10	2684.40	2900.40	3030.90	3146.40	3275.40	3360.90	3438.30	3564.30	3659.70	3659.70	3659.70	3659.70
Enlisted Members															
E-9	$0.00	$0.00	$0.00	$0.00	$0.00	$0.00	$3901.20	$3989.70	$4101.00	$4232.40	$4364.10	$4575.90	$4755.00	$4943.70	$5231.70
E-8	0.00	0.00	0.00	0.00	0.00	3193.50	3334.80	3422.10	3527.10	3640.50	3845.40	3949.20	4125.90	4224.00	4465.20
E-7	2220.00	2423.10	2515.80	2638.80	2734.50	2899.50	2992.20	3084.60	3249.60	3332.40	3410.70	3458.70	3620.40	3725.10	3990.00
E-6	1920.30	2112.60	2205.90	2296.50	2391.00	2604.30	2687.10	2779.20	2859.90	2888.70	2908.20	2908.20	2908.20	2908.20	2908.20
E-5	1759.50	1877.10	1967.70	2060.70	2205.30	2329.80	2421.60	2450.70	2450.70	2450.70	2450.70	2450.70	2450.70	2450.70	2450.70
E-4	1612.80	1695.60	1787.10	1877.70	1957.80	1957.80	1957.80	1957.80	1957.80	1957.80	1957.80	1957.80	1957.80	1957.80	1957.80
E-3	1456.20	1547.70	1641.00	1641.00	1641.00	1641.00	1641.00	1641.00	1641.00	1641.00	1641.00	1641.00	1641.00	1641.00	1641.00
E-2	1384.50	1384.50	1384.50	1384.50	1384.50	1384.50	1384.50	1384.50	1384.50	1384.50	1384.50	1384.50	1384.50	1384.50	1384.50
E-1	1235.17	1235.17	1235.10	1235.17	1235.17	1235.10	1235.10	1235.10	1235.17	1235.17	1235.10	1235.17	1235.17	1235.10	1235.10

E-1 with less than 4 months of service $1142.70

before that discussion can go very far, you will have to be tested to see, first, if you can enlist, and second, what specialties you qualify for. That's where your trip to the Military Entrance Processing Station (MEPS) comes in.

▶ Military Entrance Processing Station (MEPS)

Your recruiter will schedule you for a trip to a MEPS in your area—there is one in almost every state—for a day of written and physical testing. You will travel as a guest of Uncle Sam by plane, train, bus, or car, depending on how far away you live from the nearest facility. MEPS schedules may vary a little from area to area, but they all operate five days per week and are open a few Saturdays during the year. If for any reason you are required to stay overnight for testing, then the military will pay for your hotel room and meals.

The MEPS is where all applicants for every branch of the military begin the enlistment process. So, even if the Marine Corps is your future employer, you can expect to see staff wearing Navy blue, Army green, or Air Force blue. When you walk through the door, you will check in at the control desk and be sent to the liaison office for your branch of the service.

▶ Your MEPS Day at a Glance

During your day at MEPS you will go through three phases:

- mental (aptitude) testing
- medical exam
- administrative paperwork

Your schedule may vary from the one outlined here, depending on how much of the process you have completed in advance. Some applicants, for example, may have already taken the ASVAB at a Mobile Examining Team (MET) site near their hometown recruiting station.

Mental (Aptitude) Testing

Your day at MEPS will most likely begin with the ASVAB, if you haven't already taken it. (See Chapter 1, "What Is the ASVAB Core?") Don't underestimate the impact the ASVAB will have on your entry into the military. Results of the ASVAB test and the physical and mental exam you receive during the entrance process are used to determine whether or not you can join the branch of the military you prefer and which training programs you are qualified to enter.

Some MEPS are now conducting ASVAB testing by computer. The computer version of the test takes one hour and forty minutes to complete, as opposed to over two hours for the paper-and-pencil version. The computer ASVAB still consists of eight subtests, but it works a little differently than the paper version. The computer will give you the first question, and, if you get this question right, it gives you another question on the same subject—but this question is a bit harder than the first one. The questions get harder as you progress, and, after you answer a certain number correctly, the computer skips to the next subtest. So, you could get eight questions right, for example, and then the computer might go to the next subtest instead of requiring you to answer all 25 questions in that one subtest.

Most MEPS do not have enough computers to test everyone. If you notice that some applicants are taken to a room with the computer testing and the others are required to take the ASVAB with pen and paper, don't worry. Either way, the information and skills you need remain the same.

Medical Exam

Next is the medical exam. All of the doctors you will see at this point are civilians. You will see them at least three times during the day. During the first visit, you and the medical staff will thoroughly pore over your medical prescreening form, your medical history form, and all of the medical records you have been told by your recruiter to bring along. This meeting will be one-on-one.

After this meeting, you will move on to the examining room. You'll strip down to your underwear and perform a series of about 20 exercises that will let the medical staff see how your limbs and joints work. You may be with a group of other applicants of the same sex during this examination or you may be alone with the doctor.

Your third meeting with the doctor will be where you receive a routine physical. Among the procedures you can expect are:

- blood pressure evaluation
- pulse rate evaluation
- heart and lung check
- evaluation of blood and urine samples
- eye exam
- hearing exam
- height-proportional-to-weight check
- chest X-ray
- HIV test

Female applicants will be given a pelvic/rectal examination. Another woman will be present during this procedure, but otherwise this exam will be conducted in private.

After these checks, you will find out whether your physical condition is adequate. If the medical staff uncovers a problem that will keep you from joining the service, they will discuss the matter with you. In some cases the doctor may tell you that you are being disqualified at the moment, but that you can come back at a later date to try again. For example, if you are overweight, you could lose a few pounds and then come back to the MEPS for another try.

If the doctor wants to have a medical specialist examine you for some reason, you may have to stay overnight, or the doctor may schedule an appointment for a later date—at the military's expense, of course. Unless you do need to see a specialist, the medical exam should take no more than three hours.

Paperwork

The rest of your day will be taken up with administrative concerns. First you will meet with the guidance counselor for your branch of the service. He or she will take the results of your physical test, your ASVAB score, and all the other information you have provided and enter this information into a computer system. The computer will show which military jobs are best suited to you. Then you can begin asking questions about your career options. Before you leave the room you will know:

- for which jobs you are qualified
- which jobs suit your personality, abilities, and interests
- which jobs are available
- when that training is available

You will also be able to decide whether you prefer to enter the military on this very day or to go in under the Delayed Entry Program. Some applicants raise their right hand during swearing-in ceremonies at the end of the processing day, while others prefer to go home and decide what they want to do.

Either way, it's critical that you ask as many questions as possible during this visit with the counselor. Take your time, and be sure you know what you want before you go any further in the process. Be aware, though, that the seats in the popular training programs go fast. The earlier you make your decision, the more likely you will have a chance to get what you really want.

▶ Delayed Entry Programs

Delayed Entry Programs allow you to enlist with your chosen branch of the military and report for duty up to 365 days later. This is a popular program for students who are still in high school or for those who have other obligations that prevent them from leaving for Basic Training right away.

BASIC TRAINING (BY BRANCH)		
BRANCH	**LOCATION OF BASIC TRAINING FACILITY**	**LENGTH OF TRAINING**
Army	Fort Jackson, Columbia, SC; Fort Knox, Louisville, KY; Fort Leonard Wood, Waynesville, MO; Fort McClellan, Anniston, AL; Fort Sill, Lawton, OK	9 weeks
Navy	Salvage Training Center (NDSTC) in Panama City, FL	9 weeks
Air Force	Lackland Air Force Base, Lackland AFB, TX	6 weeks
Marine Corps	Marine Corps Recruit Depot (MCRD) Parris Island, Parris Island, SC,* or MCRD San Diego, San Diego, CA	13 weeks
Coast Guard	U.S. Coast Guard Training Center, Cape May, NJ	$7\frac{1}{2}$ weeks

All female Marines attend Basic at Parris Island. All men from the East Coast attend Parris Island. All men from the West Coast attend San Diego.

▶ Basic Training

Everything you have done has been leading up to this moment—the day you leave for Basic Training. You will report back to the MEPS to prepare to leave for Basic Training. If you have been in the Delayed Entry Program, you will get a last-minute mini-physical to make sure your condition is still up to par. You will also be asked about any changes that might affect your eligibility since the last time you were at MEPS. If you have been arrested or had any medical problems, now is the time to speak up.

Your orders and records will be completed at MEPS, and then you are on your way to Basic, by plane, bus, or car—it will all be at military expense. Where you train will depend on the branch of service. The Air Force, Navy, and Coast Guard each has only one training facility. The Marines has two, and the Army has quite a few because where the Army sends you will depend on the specialized training you signed up for at the MEPS.

The First Few Days

No matter which branch of service you join, the first few days of Basic are pretty much the same. You will spend time at an intake facility, where you will be assigned to a basic training unit and undergo a quick-paced introduction to your branch of the service. Your days will include:

- orientation briefings
- uniform distribution
- records processing
- I.D. card preparation
- barracks upkeep training
- drill and ceremony instruction
- physical training (PT)

You will be assigned to a group of recruits ranging from 35 to 80 people. The Navy and Coast Guard call this training group a "company," the Army and Marine Corps call it a "platoon," and the Air Force calls it a "flight." And let's not forget your supervisor for these early days of your military career—the drill instructor. This is your primary instructor throughout the day.

The Following Weeks

From the intake facility, you will go to your Basic Training site. You can expect your training day to start around 5:00 A.M. and officially end around 9:00 P.M. Most Saturdays and Sundays are light training days. You won't have much free time, and your ability to travel away from your unit on weekends will be very limited, if you get this privilege at all. In most cases you will not be eligible to take leave (vacation time) until after Basic Training, although exceptions can sometimes be made in case of family emergency.

The subjects you learn in Basic Training include:

- military courtesy
- military regulations
- military rules of conduct
- hygiene and sanitation
- organization and mission
- handling and care of weapons
- tactics and training related specifically to your service

While you are in Basic Training, you can expect plenty of physical training. Physical fitness is critical for trainees, and your drill instructor will keep tabs on your progress throughout Basic Training by giving you tests periodically. Your best bet is to start a running and weight-lifting program *the instant* you make your decision to join the military. Recruits in all branches of the service run mile after mile, perform hundreds of sit-ups and push-ups, and become closely acquainted with obstacle courses. These courses differ in appearance from facility to facility, but they all require the same things: plenty of upper body strength and overall endurance, as well as the will to succeed.

ENLISTMENT DURATIONS BY BRANCH	
BRANCH OF SERVICE	**TERMS OF ENLISTMENT**
Army	2, 3, 4, 5, or 6 years
Navy	3, 4, 5, or 6 years
Air Force	4 or 8 years
Marine Corps	3, 4, or 5 years
Coast Guard	4 or 6 years

Lifetime Opportunities

Basic Training, no matter which branch of the service you choose, is a time in your life that you will never forget. No one is promising you it will be pleasant, but during this time you will forge friendships you will keep for the rest of your life. And the opportunities you will have during and after your military service will be unparalleled. You may choose a lifetime career in the military, or you may use it as a springboard to a rewarding career in the private sector. Either way, your future starts now, and this book is designed to prepare you for it.

The Score You Need to Enlist

CHAPTER SUMMARY
To get the most out of this book, you need to know the score you need to get into the service branch of your choice. This chapter walks you step-by-step through the process of converting your scores on the practice tests in this book into the scores the military uses so you can tell whether you make the grade.

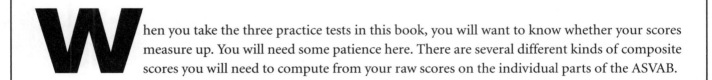

hen you take the three practice tests in this book, you will want to know whether your scores measure up. You will need some patience here. There are several different kinds of composite scores you will need to compute from your raw scores on the individual parts of the ASVAB.

▶ Calculating Your Score

Your first step is to convert the raw scores you get on your first practice exam (Chapter 5) to the scores the military uses to compute the composite score that says whether or not you can enlist. This is the Armed Forces Qualifying Test score, or AFQT.

In the table on page 14, write your scores on the Practice ASVAB Core Test 1 in the column that says "Raw Score" under Practice Test 1. Your raw score is simply the number you got right on that subtest. For the raw score in the last blank, Verbal Equivalent, add together your raw scores on both the Word Knowledge (WK) and Paragraph Comprehension (PC) subtests.

Note that blanks are also provided for Practice ASVAB Core Test 2 and Practice ASVAB Core Test 3; you can fill in those blanks when you take those tests. This table will help you keep track of your improvement as you work through the practice tests in this book.

All of the score conversions throughout this chapter are approximate. Different versions of the ASVAB vary in their score conversions, and your scores on the practice tests in this book will not be exactly the same as your score on the real ASVAB. Use the exams in this book to get an *approximate* idea of where you stand and how much you are improving.

YOUR SCORES						
	PRACTICE TEST 1		PRACTICE TEST 2		PRACTICE TEST 3	
Subtest	Raw Score	Scaled Score	Raw Score	Scaled Score	Raw Score	Scaled Score
Arithmetic Reasoning (AR)						
Word Knowledge (WK)						
Paragraph Comprehension (PC)						
Mathematics Knowledge (MK)						
Verbal Equivalent (VE = WK + PC)						

Now you need to fill in the column on the "Your Scores" table labeled "Scaled Score." Below is a table that shows you approximate correlations between raw scores and scaled scores for each subtest. On the left are raw scores. The other columns show the equivalent scaled score for each test. Make sure you're using the column for the proper subtest. The subtests are labeled with the abbreviations shown in the left-hand column of the table on page 14.

RAW SCORE TO SCALED SCORE CONVERSION					
RAW	AR	WK	PC	MK	VE
0–1	26	30	20	20	20
2–3	29	33	23	21	20
4–5	32	36	28	22	21
6–7	34	39	35	25	22
8–9	37	42	41	28	23
10–11	39	45	48	30	25
12–13	42	48	54	33	27
14–15	45	51	60	35	29
16–17	48	54		38	31
18–19	50	57		40	32
20–21	53	61		43	34
22–23	56	64		46	36
24–25	60	67		48	38
26–27	61			50	40
28–29	63			53	42
30–31	66			55	44
32–33				58	45
34–35				61	47
36–37					49
38–39					50
40					52

Find the subtest you want to score in the boxes on the top. Then, on the left column, find your raw score for that subtest. Follow the raw-score row to the right until you get to the proper subtest. That number is your scaled score for this subtest.

► Do You Qualify?

Now that you have your scaled score for each subtest filled in on the table on page 14, you are ready for the next step: finding out if your score will get you into the military. Remember to use only your *scaled scores*, not your raw scores, for these conversions.

The Armed Forces Qualifying Test (AFQT) Score

All branches of the military compute your AFQT score—the one that determines whether or not you can enlist—in the same way. Only the Verbal Equivalent (which you determined by adding Word Knowledge and Paragraph Comprehension scores and then converting to a scaled score), Arithmetic Reasoning, and Mathematics Knowledge scaled scores count toward your AFQT. The military just wants to know if you have basic reading and arithmetic skills. The score conversion goes like this:

$$2(VE) + AR + MK = AFQT$$

In other words, your AFQT (scaled score) is your Verbal Equivalent scaled score, doubled, added to your Arithmetic Reasoning and Mathematics Knowledge scaled scores. Fill in the blanks below to find your AFQT on Practice Test 1.

VE score _____ × 2 = _____

AR score _____

MK score + _____

AFQT Scaled Score _____

There's one last step. Take the AFQT scaled score and find it in the column labeled "Standard Score" on the next page. Look up the corresponding "Percentile" score. This is approximately equivalent to the score the military will use.

The Army requires a minimum AFQT score of 31 to qualify for enlistment. Marine Corps recruits must score at least 32. Navy recruits must score at least 35 on the AFQT; the Coast Guard requires a minimum of 40; and if you are going into the Air Force, you may need a score around 40. Check with your recruiter for any changes to this requirement.

If your AFQT on the first practice test isn't up to 31, don't despair. You are using this book to help you improve your score, after all, and you have just gotten started. Remember, too, that your score on these practice exams may not be exactly the same as your score on the actual test.

On the other hand, a higher score makes you more attractive to recruiters, and depending on your score on individual subtests, it may qualify you for more of the occupational specialties you want.

Use the following table to convert your AFQT scaled score to the AFQT percentile score. After you have figured out your scaled score using the formula on this page, find it on the table that follows to see what your AFQT percentile score is. This will tell you if you have received the minimum score, 31, to enlist into the Army.

AFQT SCALED SCORE TO PERCENTILE CONVERSION

STANDARD SCORE	PERCENTILE	STANDARD SCORE	PERCENTILE	STANDARD SCORE	PERCENTILE
80–120	1	186	34	221	67
121–124	2	187–188	35	222	68
125–127	3	189	36	223	69
128–131	4	190	37	224	70
132–134	5	191	38	225	71
135–137	6	192	39	226	72
138–139	7	193	40	227	73
140–142	8	194	41	228	74
143–144	9	195	42	229	75
145–146	10	196	43	230	76
147–148	11	197	44	231	77
149–150	12	198	45	232	78
151–153	13	199	46	233	79
154	14	200	47	234–235	80
155–156	15	201	48	236	81
157–158	16	202	49	237	82
159–160	17	203	50	238	83
161–162	18	204	51	239	84
163–164	19	205	52	240	85
165	20	206	53	241	86
166–167	21	207–208	54	242	87
168–169	22	209	55	243	88
170–171	23	210	56	244	89
172	24	211	57	245	90
173–174	25	212	58	246	91
175	26	213	59	247	92
176–177	27	214	60	248	93
178	28	215	61	249	94
179–180	29	216	62	250	95
181	30	217	63	251	96
182	31	218	64	252	97
183–184	32	219	65	253	98
185	33	220	66	254–320	99

The LearningExpress Test Preparation System

CHAPTER SUMMARY

Taking the ASVAB can be tough. It demands a lot of preparation if you want to achieve a top score. Whether or not you get into the military depends on how well you do on the AFQT portion of the exam. The LearningExpress Test Preparation System, developed exclusively for LearningExpress by leading test experts, gives you the discipline and attitude you need to be a winner.

▶ Getting Ready for the ASVAB

Fact: Taking the ASVAB isn't easy, and neither is getting ready for it. Your future military career depends on you passing the core section of the ASVAB—Arithmetic Reasoning, Word Knowledge, Paragraph Comprehension, and Mathematics Knowledge. By focusing on these four subtests, you have taken your first step to getting into the military. However, there are all sorts of pitfalls that can prevent you from doing your best on this all-important portion of the exam. Here are some of the obstacles that can stand in the way of your success:

- being unfamiliar with the format of the exam
- being paralyzed by test anxiety
- leaving your preparation to the last minute
- not preparing at all!
- not knowing vital test-taking skills: how to pace yourself through the exam, how to use the process of elimination, and when to guess
- not being in tip-top mental and physical shape
- messing up on test day by arriving late at the test site, having to work on an empty stomach, or shivering through the exam because the room is cold

What is the common denominator in all these test-taking pitfalls? One word: *control.* Who is in control, you or the exam?

Here is some good news: The LearningExpress Test Preparation System puts you in control. In just nine easy-to-follow steps, you will learn everything you need to know to make sure that you are in charge of your preparation and your performance on the exam. Other test takers may let the test get the better of them; other test takers may be unprepared or out of shape, but not you. You will have taken all the steps you need to take to get a passing AFQT score.

Here's how the LearningExpress Test Preparation System works: Nine easy steps lead you through everything you need to know and do to get ready to master your exam. Each of the steps listed below includes both reading about the step and one or more activities. It's important that you do the activities along with the reading, or you won't be getting the full benefit of the system. Each step tells you approximately how much time that step will take you to complete.

Step 1. Get Information	30 minutes
Step 2. Conquer Test Anxiety	20 minutes
Step 3. Make a Plan	50 minutes
Step 4. Learn to Manage Your Time	10 minutes
Step 5. Learn to Use the Process of Elimination	20 minutes
Step 6. Know When to Guess	20 minutes
Step 7. Reach Your Peak Performance Zone	10 minutes
Step 8. Get Your Act Together	10 minutes
Step 9. Do It!	10 minutes
Total	**3 hours**

We estimate that working through the entire system will take you approximately three hours, though it's perfectly OK if you work faster or slower than the time estimates assume. If you can take a whole afternoon or evening, you can work through the whole LearningExpress Test Preparation System in one sitting. Otherwise, you can break it up, and do just one or two steps a day for the next several days. It's up to you—remember, you are in control.

► Step 1: Get Information

Time to complete: 30 minutes
Activity: Read Chapter 1, "What Is the ASVAB Core?"
Knowledge is power. The first step in the LearningExpress Test Preparation System is finding out everything you can about the ASVAB core. Once you have your information, the next steps in the LearningExpress Test Preparation System will show you what to do about it.

Part A: Straight Talk about the ASVAB

Basically, the U.S. military invented the whole idea of standardized testing, starting around the time of World War I. The Department of Defense wanted to make sure that its recruits were trainable—not that they already knew the skills they needed to serve in the armed forces, but that they could learn them.

The ASVAB started as an intelligence test, but now it is a test of specific aptitudes and abilities. While some of these aptitudes, such as reading and math problem-solving skills, are important in almost any job, others, such as electronics or automotive principles, are quite specialized. These more specialized subtests don't count toward your Armed Forces Qualifying Test (AFQT) score, which determines your eligibility to enlist in the military. Only the four subtests covered in this book count toward the AFQT score.

It's important for you to realize that your score on the AFQT does not determine what kind of person you are. There are all kinds of things a written exam like this can't test: whether you can follow orders, whether you can become part of a unit that works together to accomplish a task, and so on. Those kinds of things are hard to evaluate, while a test is easy to evaluate.

This is not to say that the exam is not important! Your chances of getting into the military still depend on your getting a good score on the subtests of the ASVAB core. And that's why you're here—using the LearningExpress Test Preparation System to achieve control over the exam.

Part B: What Is on the Test

If you haven't already done so, stop here and read Chapter 1 of this book, which gives you an overview of the ASVAB core.

▶ Step 2: Conquer Test Anxiety

Time to complete: 20 minutes
Activity: Take the Test Stress Test

Having complete information about the exam is the first step in getting control of the exam. Next, you have to overcome one of the biggest obstacles to test success: test anxiety. Test anxiety not only impairs your performance on the exam itself; but also keeps you from preparing! In Step 2, you will learn stress management techniques that will help you succeed on your exam. Learn these strategies now, and practice them as you work through the exams in this book, so they will be second nature to you by exam day.

Combating Test Anxiety

The first thing you need to know is that a little test anxiety is a good thing. Everyone gets nervous before a big exam—and if that nervousness motivates you to prepare thoroughly, so much the better. It's said that Sir Laurence Olivier, one of the foremost British actors of last century, felt ill before every performance. His stage fright didn't impair his performance; in fact, it probably gave him a little extra edge—just the kind of edge you need to do well, whether on a stage or in an examination room.

On page 23 is the Test Stress Test. Stop and answer the questions to find out whether your level of test anxiety is something you should worry about.

Stress Management before the Test

If you feel your level of anxiety getting the best of you in the weeks before the test, here is what you need to do to bring the level down again:

- **Get prepared.** There is nothing like knowing what to expect and being prepared for it to put you in control of test anxiety. That's why you're reading this book. Use it faithfully, and remind yourself that you are better prepared than most of the people taking the test.

- **Practice self-confidence.** A positive attitude is a great way to combat test anxiety. This is no time to be humble or shy. Stand in front of the mirror and say to your reflection, "I'm prepared. I'm full of self-confidence. I'm going to ace this test. I know I can do it." Say it into a tape recorder and play it back once a day. If you hear it often enough, you will believe it.
- **Fight negative messages.** Every time someone starts telling you how hard the exam is or how it's almost impossible to get a high score, start telling them your self-confidence messages. Don't listen to the negative messages. Turn on your tape recorder and listen to your self-confidence messages.
- **Visualize.** Imagine yourself reporting for duty on your first day as a military trainee. Think of yourself wearing your uniform and learning skills you will use for the rest of your life. Visualizing success can help make it happen—and it reminds you of why you are going to all this work in preparing for the exam.
- **Exercise.** Physical activity helps calm your body down and focus your mind. Besides, being in good physical shape can actually help you do well on the exam. Go for a run, lift weights, go swimming—and do it regularly.

Stress Management on Test Day

There are several ways you can bring down your level of test anxiety on test day. They will work best if you practice them in the weeks before the test, so you know which ones work best for you.

- **Deep breathing.** Take a deep breath while you count to five. Hold it for a count of one, then let it out on a count of five. Repeat several times.
- **Move your body.** Try rolling your head in a circle. Rotate your shoulders. Shake your hands from the wrist. Many people find these movements very relaxing.

- **Visualize again.** Think of the place where you are most relaxed: lying on a beach in the sun, walking through the park, or whatever. Now close your eyes and imagine you are actually there. If you practice in advance, you will find that you only need a few seconds of this exercise to experience a significant increase in your sense of well-being.

When anxiety threatens to overwhelm you right there during the exam, there are still things you can do to manage the stress level:

- **Repeat your self-confidence messages.** You should have them memorized by now. Say them silently to yourself, and believe them!
- **Visualize one more time.** This time, visualize yourself moving smoothly and quickly through the test answering every question correctly and finishing just before time is up. Like most visualization techniques, this one works best if you have practiced it ahead of time.
- **Find an easy question.** Skim over the test until you find an easy question, and answer it. Getting even one question finished gets you into the test-taking groove.
- **Take a mental break.** Everyone loses concentration once in a while during a long test. It's normal, so you shouldn't worry about it. Instead, accept what has happened. Say to yourself, "Hey, I lost it there for a minute. My brain is taking a break." Put down your pencil, close your eyes, and do some deep breathing for a few seconds. Then you're ready to go back to work.

Try these techniques ahead of time, and see if they work for you!

You only need to worry about test anxiety if it is extreme enough to impair your performance. The following questionnaire will provide a diagnosis of your level of test anxiety. In the blank before each statement, write the number that most accurately describes your experience.

0 = Never   1 = Once or twice   2 = Sometimes   3 = Often

_____ I have gotten so nervous before an exam that I simply put down the books and didn't study for it.

_____ I have experienced disabling physical symptoms such as vomiting and severe headaches because I was nervous about an exam.

_____ I have simply not showed up for an exam because I was scared to take it.

_____ I have experienced dizziness and disorientation while taking an exam.

_____ I have had trouble filling in the little circles because my hands were shaking too hard.

_____ I have failed an exam because I was too nervous to complete it.

_____ **Total: Add up the numbers in the blanks above.**

Your Test Stress Score

Here are the steps you should take, depending on your score. If you scored:

- **Below 3,** your level of test anxiety is nothing to worry about; it's probably just enough to give you that little extra edge.
- **Between 3 and 6,** your test anxiety may be enough to impair your performance, and you should practice the stress management techniques listed in this section to try to bring your test anxiety down to manageable levels.
- **Above 6,** your level of test anxiety is a serious concern. In addition to practicing the stress management techniques listed in this section, you may want to seek additional, personal help. Call your community college and ask for the academic counselor. Tell the counselor that you have a level of test anxiety that sometimes keeps you from being able to take an exam. The counselor may be willing to help you or may suggest someone else you should talk to.

► Step 3: Make a Plan

Time to complete: 50 minutes
Activity: Construct a study plan

Maybe the most important thing you can do to get control of yourself and your exam is to make a study plan. Too many people fail to prepare simply because they fail to plan. Spending hours on the day before the exam poring over sample test questions not only raises your level of test anxiety, it also is simply no substitute for careful preparation and practice over time.

On the following pages are two sample schedules, based on the amount of time you have before you take the ASVAB. If you are the kind of person who needs deadlines and assignments to motivate you for a project, here they are. If you are the kind of person who doesn't like to follow other people's plans, you can use the suggested schedules here to construct your own.

Even more important than making a plan is making a commitment. You can't improve your skills in the four areas tested on the ASVAB core overnight. You have to set aside some time every day for study and practice. Try for at least 30 minutes a day. Thirty minutes daily will do you much more good than two hours on Saturday.

Don't put off your study until the day before the exam. Start now. A few minutes a day, with half an hour or more on weekends, can make a big difference in your score.

▶ Step 4: Learn to Manage Your Time

Time to complete: 10 minutes to read, many hours of practice!

Activities: Practice these strategies as you take the sample tests in this book

Steps 4, 5, and 6 of the LearningExpress Test Preparation System put you in charge of your exam by showing you test-taking strategies that work. Practice these strategies as you take the sample tests in this book, and then you will be ready to use them on test day.

First, you will take control of your time on the exam. Each of the four subtests of the ASVAB core is timed separately. Most allow you enough time to complete the section, though none allows a lot of extra time. You should use your time wisely to avoid making errors. Here are some general tips for the whole exam.

- **Listen carefully to directions.** By the time you get to the exam, you should know how all the subtests work, but listen just in case something has changed.
- **Pace yourself.** Glance at your watch every few minutes, and compare the time to how far you have gotten in the subtest. When one-quarter of the time has elapsed, you should be one-quarter of the way through the subtest, and so on. If you're falling behind, pick up the pace a bit.
- **Keep moving.** Don't dither around on one question. If you don't know the answer, skip the question and move on. Circle the number of the question in your test booklet in case you have time to come back to it later.
- **Keep track of your place on the answer sheet.** If you skip a question, make sure you skip on the answer sheet too. Check yourself every 5–10 questions to make sure the question number and the answer sheet number are still the same.
- **Don't rush.** Though you should keep moving, rushing won't help. Try to keep calm and work methodically and quickly.

Schedule A: The Two-Week Plan

If you have at least two weeks before you take the ASVAB, you have plenty of time to prepare—as long as you don't waste it! If you have less than two weeks, turn to Schedule B.

TIME	PREPARATION
Day 1	Take the first practice exam in Chapter 5. Score the exam and identify two areas that you will concentrate on before you take the second practice exam.
Days 2–5	Study the areas you identified as your weaknesses. Don't forget, there are review lessons and practice questions for Math, Reading, and Vocabulary in Chapters 6–11. Review these chapters in detail to improve your score on the next practice test.

Day 6	Take the second practice exam in Chapter 12 and calculate your score. Identify one area to concentrate on before you take the third practice exam.
Days 7–9	Study the one area you identified for further review. Again, use the Math, Reading, and Vocabulary chapters for help.
Day 10	Take the last practice exam in Chapter 13. Score the test. Note how much you have improved!
Days 11–13	Take an overview of all your study materials, consolidating your strengths and improving on your weaknesses.
Day before the exam	Relax. Do something unrelated to the exam and go to bed at a reasonable hour.

Schedule B: The One-Week Plan

If you have a week or less before you take the exam, use this seven-day schedule to help you make the most of your time.

TIME	PREPARATION
Day 1	Take the first practice exam in Chapter 5 and review the answers and explanations. Note which topics you need to review most.
Day 2	Review one area that gave you trouble on the first practice exam. Use the review lessons and practice questions in Chapters 6–11 to hone your skills.
Day 3	Take the second practice exam in Chapter 12 and score it.
Day 4	If your score on the second practice exam doesn't show improvement on the two areas you studied, continue to use the review chapters to improve some skills and reinforce others. If you did improve in those areas, choose a new weak area to study today.
Day 5	Take the third practice exam in Chapter 13 and score it. See how much you have improved since the first practice test!
Day 6	Use your last study day to brush up on any areas that are still giving you trouble. Use the review and practice chapters.
Day before the exam	Relax. Do something unrelated to the exam and go to bed at a reasonable hour.

▶ Step 5: Learn to Use the Process of Elimination

Time to complete: 20 minutes
Activity: Complete worksheet on Using the Process of Elimination

After time management, your next most important tool for taking control of your exam is using the process of elimination wisely. It's standard test-taking wisdom that you should always read all the answer choices before choosing your answer. This helps you find the right answer by eliminating wrong answer choices. And, sure enough, that standard wisdom applies to your exam, too.

You should always use the process of elimination on tough questions, even if the right answer jumps out at you. Sometimes the answer that jumps out isn't right after all. You should always proceed through the answer choices in order. You can start with answer choice **a** and eliminate any choices that are clearly incorrect.

Let's say you're facing a vocabulary question that goes like this:

"Biology uses a <u>binomial</u> system of classification." In this sentence, the word <u>binomial</u> most nearly means
a. understanding the law.
b. having two names.
c. scientifically sound.
d. having a double meaning.

If you happen to know what *binomial* means, of course, you don't need to use the process of elimination, but let's assume you don't. So, you look at the answer choices. "understanding the law" sure doesn't sound very likely for something having to do with biology. So you eliminate choice **a**—and now you only have three answer choices to deal with. Mark an X next to choice **a** so you never have to read it again.

Now, move on to the other answer choices. If you know that the prefix *bi-* means *two*, as in *bicycle*, you will flag answer **b** as a possible answer. Mark a check mark beside it, meaning "good answer, I might use this one."

Choice **c**, "scientifically sound," is a possibility. At least it's about science, not law. It could work here, though, when you think about it, having a "scientifically sound" classification system in a scientific field is kind of redundant. You remember the *bi* in *binomial,* and probably continue to like answer **b** better. But you're not sure, so you put a question mark next to **c**, meaning "well, maybe."

Now, choice **d**, "having a double meaning." You're still keeping in mind that *bi-* means *two,* so this one looks possible at first. But then you look again at the sentence the word belongs in, and you think, "Why would biology want a system of classification that has two meanings? That wouldn't work very well!" If you're really taken with the idea that *bi* means *two,* you might put a question mark here. But if you're feeling a little more confident, you'll put an X. You have already got a better answer picked out.

Now your question looks like this:

"Biology uses a <u>binomial</u> system of classification." In this sentence, the word <u>binomial</u> most nearly means
X **a.** understanding the law.
✓ **b.** having two names.
? **c.** scientifically sound.
? **d.** having a double meaning.

You've got just one checkmark for a good answer. If you're pressed for time, you should simply mark answer **b** on your answer sheet. If you have the time to be extra careful, you could compare your check-mark answer to your question-mark answers to make sure that it's better. (It is: The *binomial* system in biology is the one that gives a two-part genus and species name like *homo sapiens.*)

It's good to have a system for marking good, bad, and maybe answers. Here's one recommendation:

X = bad
✓ = good
? = maybe

If you don't like these marks, devise your own system. Just make sure you do it long before test day—while you're working through the practice exams in this book—so you won't have to worry about it during the test.

Even when you think you are absolutely clueless about a question, you can often use the process of elimination to get rid of one answer choice. If so, you are better prepared to make an educated guess, as you will see in Step 6. More often, the process of elimination allows you to get down to only *two* possibly right answers. Then, you're in a strong position to guess.

And sometimes, even though you don't know the right answer, you find it simply by getting rid of the wrong ones, as you did in the previous example.

Try using your powers of elimination on the questions in the worksheet "Using the Process of Elimination" that follows. The answer explanations there show one possible way you might use the process to arrive at the right answer.

The process of elimination is your tool for the next step, which is knowing when to guess.

Using the Process of Elimination

Use the process of elimination to answer the following questions.

1. Ilsa is as old as Meghan will be in five years. The difference between Ed's age and Meghan's age is twice the difference between Ilsa's age and Meghan's age. Ed is 29. How old is Ilsa?
  a. 4
  b. 10
  c. 19
  d. 24

2. "All drivers of commercial vehicles must carry a valid commercial driver's license whenever operating a commercial vehicle." According to this sentence, which of the following people need NOT carry a commercial driver's license?
  a. a truck driver idling his engine while waiting to be directed to a loading dock
  b. a bus operator backing her bus out of the way of another bus in the bus lot
  c. a taxi driver driving his personal car to the grocery store
  d. a limousine driver taking the limousine to her home after dropping off her last passenger of the evening

3. Smoking tobacco has been linked to
  a. increased risk of stroke and heart attack.
  b. all forms of respiratory disease.
  c. increasing mortality rates over the past ten years.
  d. juvenile delinquency.

4. Which of the following words is spelled correctly?
  a. incorrigible
  b. outragous
  c. domestickated
  d. understandible

Answers

Here are the answers, as well as some suggestions as to how you might have used the process of elimination to find them.

1. d. You should have eliminated answer **a** off the bat. Ilsa can't be four years old if Meghan is going to be Ilsa's age in five years. The best way to eliminate other answer choices is to try plugging them in to the information given in the problem. For instance, for answer **b**, if Ilsa is 10, then Meghan must be 5. The difference in their ages is 5. The difference between Ed's age, 29, and Meghan's age, 5, is 24. Is 24 two times 5? No. Then answer **b** is wrong. You could eliminate answer **c** in the same way and be left with answer **d**.

2. c. Note the word *not* in the question, and go through the answers one by one. Is the truck driver in choice **a** "operating a commercial vehicle"? Yes, idling counts as "operating," so he needs to have a commercial driver's license. Likewise, the bus operator in answer **b** is operating a commercial vehicle; the question doesn't say the operator has to be on the street. The limo driver in **d** is operating a commercial vehicle, even if it doesn't have passenger in it. However, the cabbie in answer **c** is *not* operating a commercial vehicle, but his own private car.

3. a. You could eliminate answer **b** simply because of the presence of the word *all*. Such absolutes hardly ever appear in correct answer choices. Choice **c** looks attractive until you think a little about what you know—aren't fewer people smoking these days, rather than more? So how could smoking be responsible for a higher mortality rate? (If you didn't know that *mortality rate* means the rate at which people die, you might keep this choice as a possibility, but you'd still be able to eliminate two answers and have only two to choose from.) Choice **d** is plain silly, so you could eliminate that one, too. You're left with the correct choice, **a**.

4. a. How you used the process of elimination here depends on which words you recognized as being spelled incorrectly. If you knew that the correct spellings were *outrageous, domesticated,* and *understandable,* then you were home free. You probably knew that at least one of those words was wrong!

► Step 6: Know When to Guess

Time to complete: 20 minutes
Activity: Complete worksheet on Your Guessing Ability

Armed with the process of elimination, you are ready to take control of one of the big questions in test-taking: Should I guess? The first and main answer is Yes. Some exams have what is called a "guessing penalty," in which a fraction of your wrong answers is subtracted from your right answers—but the ASVAB isn't one of them. The number of questions you answer correctly yields your raw score. So you have nothing to lose and everything to gain by guessing.

The more complicated answer to the question "Should I guess?" depends on you—your personality and your "guessing intuition." There are two things you need to know about yourself before you go into the exam:

- Are you a risk-taker?
- Are you a good guesser?

You will have to decide about your risk-taking quotient on your own. To find out if you're a good guesser, complete the following worksheet "Your Guessing Ability." Frankly, even if you're a play-it-safe person with lousy intuition, you are still safe in guessing every time. The best thing would be if you could overcome your anxieties and go ahead and mark an answer. But you may want to have a sense of how good your intuition is before you go into the exam.

Your Guessing Ability

The following are ten really hard questions. You are not supposed to know the answers. Rather, this is an assessment of your ability to guess when you don't have a clue. Read each question carefully, just as if you did expect to answer it. If you have any knowledge at all about the subject of the question, use that knowledge to help you eliminate wrong answer choices.

ANSWER GRID

1. ⓐ ⓑ ⓒ ⓓ	**5.** ⓐ ⓑ ⓒ ⓓ	**9.** ⓐ ⓑ ⓒ ⓓ
2. ⓐ ⓑ ⓒ ⓓ	**6.** ⓐ ⓑ ⓒ ⓓ	**10.** ⓐ ⓑ ⓒ ⓓ
3. ⓐ ⓑ ⓒ ⓓ	**7.** ⓐ ⓑ ⓒ ⓓ	
4. ⓐ ⓑ ⓒ ⓓ	**8.** ⓐ ⓑ ⓒ ⓓ	

1. September 7 is Independence Day in
   a. India.
   b. Costa Rica.
   c. Brazil.
   d. Australia.

2. Which of the following is the formula for determining the momentum of an object?
   a. $p = mv$
   b. $F = ma$
   c. $P = IV$
   d. $E = mc^2$

3. Because of the expansion of the universe, the stars and other celestial bodies are all moving away from each other. This phenomenon is known as
   a. Newton's first law.
   b. the big bang.
   c. gravitational collapse.
   d. Hubble flow.

4. American author Gertrude Stein was born in
   a. 1713.
   b. 1830.
   c. 1874.
   d. 1901.

5. Which of the following is NOT one of the Five Classics attributed to Confucius?
   a. the *I Ching*
   b. the *Book of Holiness*
   c. the *Spring and Autumn Annals*
   d. the *Book of History*

6. The religious and philosophical doctrine that holds that the universe is constantly in a struggle between good and evil is known as
   a. Pelagianism.
   b. Manichaeanism.
   c. neo-Hegelianism.
   d. Epicureanism.

7. The third Chief Justice of the U.S. Supreme Court was
   a. John Blair.
   b. William Cushing.
   c. James Wilson.
   d. John Jay.

8. Which of the following is the poisonous portion of a daffodil?
   a. the bulb
   b. the leaves
   c. the stem
   d. the flowers

9. The winner of the Masters golf tournament in 1953 was
   a. Sam Snead.
   b. Cary Middlecoff.
   c. Arnold Palmer.
   d. Ben Hogan.

10. The state with the highest per capita personal income in 1980 was
   a. Alaska.
   b. Connecticut.
   c. New York.
   d. Texas.

Answers

Check your answers against the correct answers below.

1. c.
2. a.
3. d.
4. c.
5. b.
6. b.
7. b.
8. a.
9. d.
10. a.

How Did You Do?

You may have simply gotten lucky and actually known the answer to one or two questions. In addition, your guessing was more successful if you were able to use the process of elimination on any of the questions. Maybe you didn't know who the third Chief Justice was (question 7), but you knew that John Jay was the first. In that case, you would have eliminated answer **d** and therefore improved your odds of guessing correctly from one in four to one in three.

According to probability, you should get $2\frac{1}{2}$ answers correct, so getting either two or three right would be average. If you got four or more right, you may be a really terrific guesser. If you got one or none right, you may be a really bad guesser.

Keep in mind, though, that this is only a small sample. You should continue to keep track of your guessing ability as you work through the sample questions in this book. Circle the numbers of questions you guess on as you make your guess; or, if you don't have time while you take the practice exams, go back afterward and try to remember which questions you guessed at. Remember, on an exam with four answer choices, your chances of getting a right answer is one in four. So keep a separate "guessing" score for each exam. How many questions did you guess on? How many did you get right? If the number you got right is at least one-fourth of the number of questions you guessed on, you are at least an average guesser, maybe better—and you should always go ahead and guess on a real exam.

► Step 7: Reach Your Peak Performance Zone

Time to complete: 10 minutes to read; weeks to complete!
Activity: Complete the Physical Preparation Checklist

To get ready for a challenge like a big exam, you have to take control of your physical, as well as your mental, state. Exercise, proper diet, and rest will ensure that your body works with, rather than against, your mind on test day, as well as during your preparation.

Exercise

If you don't already have a regular exercise program going, the time during which you are preparing for an exam is actually an excellent time to start one. You will have to be pretty fit to make it through the first weeks of Basic Training anyway. And if you're already keeping fit—or trying to get that way—don't let the pressure of preparing for an exam fool you into quitting now. Exercise helps reduce stress by pumping wonderful good-feeling hormones called endorphins into your system. It also increases the oxygen supply throughout your body, including your brain, so you will be at peak performance on test day.

A half hour of vigorous activity—enough to raise a sweat—every day should be your aim. If you are really pressed for time, every other day is OK. Choose an activity you like and get out there and do it. Jogging with a friend always makes the time go faster, or take a radio.

But don't overdo it. You don't want to exhaust yourself. Moderation is the key.

Diet

First of all, cut out the junk. Go easy on caffeine and nicotine, and eliminate alcohol and any other drugs from your system at least two weeks before the exam. Promise yourself a treat the night after the exam, if need be.

What your body needs for peak performance is simply a balanced diet. Eat plenty of fruits and vegetables, along with protein and carbohydrates. Foods that are high in lecithin (an amino acid), such as fish and beans, are especially good brain foods.

The night before the exam, you might "carbo-load" the way athletes do before a contest. Eat a big plate of spaghetti, rice and beans, or whatever your favorite carbohydrate is.

Rest

You probably know how much sleep you need every night to be at your best, even if you don't always get it. Make sure you do get that much sleep, though, for at least a week before the exam. Moderation is important here, too. Extra sleep will just make you groggy.

If you are not a morning person and your exam will be given in the morning, you should reset your internal clock so that your body doesn't think you're taking an exam at 3:00 A.M. You have to start this process well before the exam. The way it works is to get up half an hour earlier each morning, and then go to bed half an hour earlier that night. Don't try it the other way around. You will just toss and turn if you go to bed early without having gotten up early. The next morning, get up another half an hour earlier, and so on. How long you will have to do this depends on how late you're used to getting up. Use the Physical Preparation Checklist on page 33 to make sure you are in tip-top form.

▶ Step 8: Get Your Act Together

Time to complete: 10 minutes to read;
                time to complete will vary
Activity: Complete Final Preparations worksheet
You are in control of your mind and body; you are in charge of test anxiety, your preparation, and your test-taking strategies. Now it's time to take charge of external factors, like the testing site and the materials you need to take the exam.

Getting to the MEPS

You will be the guest of the Department of Defense in your trip to the Military Entrance Processing Station (MEPS). You will probably be scheduled to spend a full day at the MEPS, though if it's far from your hometown, you may have to go the night before. Your recruiter will tell you when and where you will be picked up for your trip to the MEPS. Make sure you know how to get to that location, if it's not your recruiting station, and how long it will take to get there. Figure out how early you will have to get up that morning, and get up that early every day for a week before your MEPS day.

Gather Your Materials

The night before the exam, lay out the clothes you will wear and the materials you have to bring with you to the MEPS. Plan on dressing in layers; you won't have any control over the temperature of the examination room. Have a sweater or jacket you can take off if it's warm. Use the checklist on the Final Preparations worksheet on page 34 to help you pull together what you will need.

Don't Skip Breakfast

Even if you don't usually eat breakfast, do so on exam morning. A cup of coffee doesn't count. Don't do doughnuts or other sweet foods, either. A sugar high will leave you with a sugar low in the middle of the exam. A mix of protein and carbohydrates is best: cereal with milk and just a little sugar, or eggs with toast, will do your body a world of good.

▶ Step 9: Do It!

Time to complete: 10 minutes, plus test-taking time
Activity: Ace the ASVAB core!
Fast forward to exam day. You are ready. You made a study plan and followed through. You practiced your test-taking strategies while working through this book. You are in control of your physical, mental, and emotional state. You know when and where to show up and what to bring with you. In other words, you are better prepared than most of the other people taking the ASVAB with you. You are psyched.

Just one more thing. When you're done with your day at the MEPS, you will have earned a reward. Plan a celebration. Call up your friends and plan a party, or have a nice dinner for two—whatever your heart desires. Give yourself something to look forward to.

And then do it. Take the ASVAB, full of confidence, armed with the test-taking strategies you have practiced until they are second nature. You are in control of yourself, your environment, and your performance on the exam. You are ready to succeed. So do it. Go in there and ace the exam. And look forward to your future military career!

Physical Preparation Checklist

For the week before the test, write down 1) what physical exercise you engaged in and for how long and 2) what you ate for each meal. Remember, you're trying for at least half an hour of exercise every other day (preferably every day) and a balanced diet that's light on junk food.

Exam minus 7 days

Exercise: _____ for _____ minutes

Breakfast: _____

Lunch: _____

Dinner: _____

Snacks: _____

Exam minus 6 days

Exercise: _____ for _____ minutes

Breakfast: _____

Lunch: _____

Dinner: _____

Snacks: _____

Exam minus 5 days

Exercise: _____ for _____ minutes

Breakfast: _____

Lunch: _____

Dinner: _____

Snacks: _____

Exam minus 4 days

Exercise: _____ for _____ minutes

Breakfast: _____

Lunch: _____

Dinner: _____

Snacks: _____

Exam minus 3 days

Exercise: _____ for _____ minutes

Breakfast: _____

Lunch: _____

Dinner: _____

Snacks: _____

Exam minus 2 days

Exercise: _____ for _____ minutes

Breakfast: _____

Lunch: _____

Dinner: _____

Snacks: _____

Exam minus 1 day

Exercise: _____ for _____ minutes

Breakfast: _____

Lunch: _____

Dinner: _____

Snacks: _____

Getting to the MEPS Pickup Site

Location of pickup site: _____

Date: _____

Departure time: _____

Do I know how to get to the pickup site?   Yes ___   No ___

If no, make a trial run.

Time it will take to get to the pickup site: _____

Things to Lay Out the Night Before

Clothes I will wear   _____

Sweater/jacket   _____

Watch   _____

Photo ID   _____

Other   _____

CHAPTER

5 ▶ Practice ASVAB Core Test 1

CHAPTER SUMMARY

This is the first of three practice tests in this book based on the sections of the ASVAB that count towards your AFQT score. Use this test to see how you would do if you were to take the exam today.

The ASVAB consists of eight subtests. Only four of these subtests count toward your Armed Forces Qualifying Test (AFQT) score, which determines whether or not you are qualified to enlist in the military. These four subtests—Arithmetic Reasoning, Word Knowledge, Paragraph Comprehension, and Mathematics Knowledge—are included in the practice test that follows.

The amount of time allowed for each subtest will be found at the beginning of that subtest. For now, don't worry too much about timing. Just take the tests in as relaxed a manner as you can. The answer sheet you should use for answering the questions is on the page 37. Complete answer explanations follow the test.

► Part 1: Arithmetic Reasoning

1.	ⓐ	ⓑ	ⓒ	ⓓ	11.	ⓐ	ⓑ	ⓒ	ⓓ	21.	ⓐ	ⓑ	ⓒ	ⓓ
2.	ⓐ	ⓑ	ⓒ	ⓓ	12.	ⓐ	ⓑ	ⓒ	ⓓ	22.	ⓐ	ⓑ	ⓒ	ⓓ
3.	ⓐ	ⓑ	ⓒ	ⓓ	13.	ⓐ	ⓑ	ⓒ	ⓓ	23.	ⓐ	ⓑ	ⓒ	ⓓ
4.	ⓐ	ⓑ	ⓒ	ⓓ	14.	ⓐ	ⓑ	ⓒ	ⓓ	24.	ⓐ	ⓑ	ⓒ	ⓓ
5.	ⓐ	ⓑ	ⓒ	ⓓ	15.	ⓐ	ⓑ	ⓒ	ⓓ	25.	ⓐ	ⓑ	ⓒ	ⓓ
6.	ⓐ	ⓑ	ⓒ	ⓓ	16.	ⓐ	ⓑ	ⓒ	ⓓ	26.	ⓐ	ⓑ	ⓒ	ⓓ
7.	ⓐ	ⓑ	ⓒ	ⓓ	17.	ⓐ	ⓑ	ⓒ	ⓓ	27.	ⓐ	ⓑ	ⓒ	ⓓ
8.	ⓐ	ⓑ	ⓒ	ⓓ	18.	ⓐ	ⓑ	ⓒ	ⓓ	28.	ⓐ	ⓑ	ⓒ	ⓓ
9.	ⓐ	ⓑ	ⓒ	ⓓ	19.	ⓐ	ⓑ	ⓒ	ⓓ	29.	ⓐ	ⓑ	ⓒ	ⓓ
10.	ⓐ	ⓑ	ⓒ	ⓓ	20.	ⓐ	ⓑ	ⓒ	ⓓ	30.	ⓐ	ⓑ	ⓒ	ⓓ

► Part 2: Word Knowledge

1.	ⓐ	ⓑ	ⓒ	ⓓ	10.	ⓐ	ⓑ	ⓒ	ⓓ	19.	ⓐ	ⓑ	ⓒ	ⓓ
2.	ⓐ	ⓑ	ⓒ	ⓓ	11.	ⓐ	ⓑ	ⓒ	ⓓ	20.	ⓐ	ⓑ	ⓒ	ⓓ
3.	ⓐ	ⓑ	ⓒ	ⓓ	12.	ⓐ	ⓑ	ⓒ	ⓓ	21.	ⓐ	ⓑ	ⓒ	ⓓ
4.	ⓐ	ⓑ	ⓒ	ⓓ	13.	ⓐ	ⓑ	ⓒ	ⓓ	22.	ⓐ	ⓑ	ⓒ	ⓓ
5.	ⓐ	ⓑ	ⓒ	ⓓ	14.	ⓐ	ⓑ	ⓒ	ⓓ	23.	ⓐ	ⓑ	ⓒ	ⓓ
6.	ⓐ	ⓑ	ⓒ	ⓓ	15.	ⓐ	ⓑ	ⓒ	ⓓ	24.	ⓐ	ⓑ	ⓒ	ⓓ
7.	ⓐ	ⓑ	ⓒ	ⓓ	16.	ⓐ	ⓑ	ⓒ	ⓓ	25.	ⓐ	ⓑ	ⓒ	ⓓ
8.	ⓐ	ⓑ	ⓒ	ⓓ	17.	ⓐ	ⓑ	ⓒ	ⓓ					
9.	ⓐ	ⓑ	ⓒ	ⓓ	18.	ⓐ	ⓑ	ⓒ	ⓓ					

► Part 3: Paragraph Comprehension

1.	ⓐ	ⓑ	ⓒ	ⓓ	6.	ⓐ	ⓑ	ⓒ	ⓓ	11.	ⓐ	ⓑ	ⓒ	ⓓ
2.	ⓐ	ⓑ	ⓒ	ⓓ	7.	ⓐ	ⓑ	ⓒ	ⓓ	12.	ⓐ	ⓑ	ⓒ	ⓓ
3.	ⓐ	ⓑ	ⓒ	ⓓ	8.	ⓐ	ⓑ	ⓒ	ⓓ	13.	ⓐ	ⓑ	ⓒ	ⓓ
4.	ⓐ	ⓑ	ⓒ	ⓓ	9.	ⓐ	ⓑ	ⓒ	ⓓ	14.	ⓐ	ⓑ	ⓒ	ⓓ
5.	ⓐ	ⓑ	ⓒ	ⓓ	10.	ⓐ	ⓑ	ⓒ	ⓓ	15.	ⓐ	ⓑ	ⓒ	ⓓ

► Part 4: Mathematics Knowledge

1.	ⓐ	ⓑ	ⓒ	ⓓ	13.	ⓐ	ⓑ	ⓒ	ⓓ	25.	ⓐ	ⓑ	ⓒ	ⓓ
2.	ⓐ	ⓑ	ⓒ	ⓓ	14.	ⓐ	ⓑ	ⓒ	ⓓ	26.	ⓐ	ⓑ	ⓒ	ⓓ
3.	ⓐ	ⓑ	ⓒ	ⓓ	15.	ⓐ	ⓑ	ⓒ	ⓓ	27.	ⓐ	ⓑ	ⓒ	ⓓ
4.	ⓐ	ⓑ	ⓒ	ⓓ	16.	ⓐ	ⓑ	ⓒ	ⓓ	28.	ⓐ	ⓑ	ⓒ	ⓓ
5.	ⓐ	ⓑ	ⓒ	ⓓ	17.	ⓐ	ⓑ	ⓒ	ⓓ	29.	ⓐ	ⓑ	ⓒ	ⓓ
6.	ⓐ	ⓑ	ⓒ	ⓓ	18.	ⓐ	ⓑ	ⓒ	ⓓ	30.	ⓐ	ⓑ	ⓒ	ⓓ
7.	ⓐ	ⓑ	ⓒ	ⓓ	19.	ⓐ	ⓑ	ⓒ	ⓓ	31.	ⓐ	ⓑ	ⓒ	ⓓ
8.	ⓐ	ⓑ	ⓒ	ⓓ	20.	ⓐ	ⓑ	ⓒ	ⓓ	32.	ⓐ	ⓑ	ⓒ	ⓓ
9.	ⓐ	ⓑ	ⓒ	ⓓ	21.	ⓐ	ⓑ	ⓒ	ⓓ	33.	ⓐ	ⓑ	ⓒ	ⓓ
10.	ⓐ	ⓑ	ⓒ	ⓓ	22.	ⓐ	ⓑ	ⓒ	ⓓ	34.	ⓐ	ⓑ	ⓒ	ⓓ
11.	ⓐ	ⓑ	ⓒ	ⓓ	23.	ⓐ	ⓑ	ⓒ	ⓓ	35.	ⓐ	ⓑ	ⓒ	ⓓ
12.	ⓐ	ⓑ	ⓒ	ⓓ	24.	ⓐ	ⓑ	ⓒ	ⓓ					

▶ Part 1: Arithmetic Reasoning

Time: 36 minutes

1. It costs $0.75 each to make color copies at a copy center. At this price, how many copies can be purchased with $60.00?
   a. 8
   b. 45
   c. 80
   d. 75

2. An aquarium has a base length of 12 inches and a width of 5 inches. If the aquarium is 10 inches tall, what is the total volume?
   a. 480 cubic inches
   b. 540 cubic inches
   c. 600 cubic inches
   d. 720 cubic inches

3. A man turns in a woman's handbag to the Lost and Found Department of a large downtown store. The man informs the clerk in charge that he found the handbag on the floor beside an entranceway. The clerk estimates that the handbag is worth approximately $150. Inside, the clerk finds the following items:

1 leather makeup case valued at	$65
1 vial of perfume, unopened, valued at	$75
1 pair of earrings valued at	$150
cash	$178

The clerk is writing a report to be submitted along with the found property. What should he write as the total value of the found cash and property?
   a. $468
   b. $608
   c. $618
   d. $718

Use the following information to answer questions 4–6.

The cost of movie theater tickets is $7.50 for adults and $5 for children ages 12 and under. On Saturday and Sunday afternoons until 4:00 P.M., there is a matinee price: $5.50 for adults and $3 for children ages 12 and under. Special group discounts are available for groups of 30 or more people.

4. Which of these can be determined from the information given in the passage?
   a. how much it will cost a family of four to buy movie theater tickets on Saturday afternoon
   b. the difference between the cost of two movie theater tickets on Tuesday night and the cost of one ticket on Sunday at 3:00 P.M.
   c. how much movie theater tickets will cost each person if he or she is part of a group of 40 people
   d. the difference between the cost of a movie theater ticket for an adult on Friday night and a movie theater ticket for a 13-year-old on Saturday afternoon at 1:00 P.M.

5. Based on the passage, how much will movie theater tickets cost for two adults, one 15-year-old child, and one 10-year-old child at 7:00 P.M. on a Sunday night?
   a. $17.00
   b. $19.50
   c. $25.00
   d. $27.50

6. Using the passage, how can you find the difference in price between a movie theater ticket for an adult and a movie theater ticket for a child under the age of 12 if the tickets are for a show at 3:00 P.M. on a Saturday afternoon?
a. subtract $3.00 from $5.50
b. subtract $5.00 from $7.50
c. subtract $7.50 from $5.50
d. add $5.50 and $3.00 and divide by 2

7. It takes a typist 0.75 seconds to type one word. At this rate, how many words can be typed in 60 seconds?
a. 4.5
b. 8
c. 45
d. 80

8. If the average woman burns 8.2 calories per minute while riding a bicycle, how many calories will she burn if she rides for 35 minutes?
a. 286
b. 287
c. 387
d. 980

9. Dr. Drake charges $36.00 for an office visit, which is $\frac{3}{4}$ of what Dr. Jean charges. How much does Dr. Jean charge?
a. $48.00
b. $27.00
c. $38.00
d. $57.00

10. Thirty percent of the students at a middle school are involved in the vocal and instrumental music programs. If 15% of the musicians are in the choir, what percentage of the whole school is in the choir?
a. 4.5%
b. 9.0%
c. 15%
d. 30%

Use the information below to answer questions 11 and 12.

Basic cable television service, which includes 16 channels, costs $15 a month. The initial labor fee to install the service is $25. A $65 deposit is required but will be refunded within two years if the customer's bills are paid in full. Other cable services may be added to the basic service: the movie channel service is $9.40 a month; the news channels are $7.50 a month; the arts channels are $5.00 a month; the sports channels are $4.80 a month.

11. A customer's cable television bill totaled $20 a month. Using the passage above, what portion of the bill was for basic cable service?
a. 25%
b. 33%
c. 50%
d. 75%

12. A customer's first bill after having cable television installed totaled $112.50. This customer chose basic cable and one additional cable service. Which additional service was chosen?
a. the news channels
b. the movie channels
c. the arts channels
d. the sports channels

13. Out of 100 shoppers polled, 80 said they buy fresh fruit every week. How many shoppers out of 30,000 could be expected to buy fresh fruit every week?
a. 2,400
b. 6,000
c. 22,000
d. 24,000

Use the information below to answer questions 14 and 15.

Compact Discs Sold

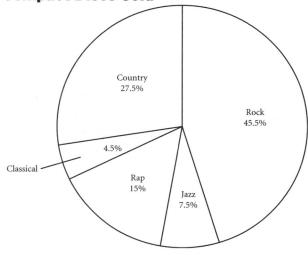

14. If 400 compact discs were sold altogether, how many of the compact discs sold were country music?
  a. 11
  b. 28
  c. 55
  d. 110

15. Based on the graph, which types of music represent exactly half of the compact discs sold?
  a. rock and jazz
  b. classical and rock
  c. rap, classical, and country
  d. jazz, classical, and rap

16. Last year, 220 people bought cars from a certain dealer. Of those, 60% reported that they were completely satisfied with their new cars. How many people reported being unsatisfied with their new car?
  a. 36
  b. 55
  c. 88
  d. 132

17. Of 1,125 university students, 135 speak fluent Spanish. What percentage of the student body speaks fluent Spanish?
  a. 7.3%
  b. 8.3%
  c. 12%
  d. 14%

18. The perimeter of a rectangle is 148 feet. Its two longest sides add up to 86 feet. What is the length of each of its two shortest sides?
  a. 31 feet
  b. 42 feet
  c. 62 feet
  d. 74 feet

19. A piece of ribbon 3 feet 4 inches long was divided in 5 equal parts. How long was each part?
  a. 1 foot 2 inches
  b. 10 inches
  c. 8 inches
  d. 6 inches

20. A middle school cafeteria has three different options for lunch.
    For $2, a student can get either a sandwich or two cookies.
    For $3, a student can get a sandwich and one cookie.
    For $4, a student can get either two sandwiches, or a sandwich and two cookies.
    If Jimae has $6 to pay for lunch for her and her brother, which of the following is not a possible combination?
  a. three sandwiches and one cookie
  b. two sandwiches and two cookies
  c. one sandwich and four cookies
  d. three sandwiches and no cookies

21. A bed is 5 feet wide and 7 feet long. What is the area of the bed?
   a. 12 square feet
   b. 22 square feet
   c. 24 square feet
   d. 35 square feet

22. Mr. Beard's temperature is 98° Fahrenheit. What is his temperature in degrees Celsius?
   $C = \frac{5}{9}(F - 32)$
   a. 35.8
   b. 36.7
   c. 37.6
   d. 31.1

23. All of the rooms on the main floor of an office building are rectangular, with 8-foot-high ceilings. Keira's office is 9 feet wide by 11 feet long. What is the combined surface area of the four walls of her office, including any windows and doors?
   a. 99 square feet
   b. 160 square feet
   c. 320 square feet
   d. 729 square feet

24. A recipe serves four people and calls for $1\frac{1}{2}$ cups of broth. If you want to serve six people, how much broth do you need?
   a. 2 cups
   b. $2\frac{1}{4}$ cups
   c. $2\frac{1}{3}$ cups
   d. $2\frac{1}{2}$ cups

25. Plattville is 80 miles west and 60 miles north of Quincy. How long is a direct route from Plattville to Quincy?
   a. 100 miles
   b. 120 miles
   c. 140 miles
   d. 160 miles

26. A builder has 27 cubic feet of concrete to pave a sidewalk whose length is 6 times its width. The concrete must be poured 6 inches deep. How long is the sidewalk?
   a. 9 feet
   b. 12 feet
   c. 15 feet
   d. 18 feet

27. Which of the following brands is the least expensive?

Brand	W	X	Y	Z
Price	0.21	0.48	0.56	0.96
Weight in ounces	6	15	20	32

   a. W
   b. X
   c. Y
   d. Z

28. A salesman drives 2,052 miles in six days, stopping at two towns each day. How many miles does he average between stops?
   a. 171
   b. 342
   c. 684
   d. 1,026

29. A cook spends $540 on silverware. If a place setting includes one knife, one fork, and two spoons, and if knives cost twice as much as forks or spoons, how many place settings did the cook buy?
   a. 90
   b. 108
   c. 135
   d. 180

30. An office uses two dozen pencils and $3\frac{1}{2}$ reams of paper each week. If pencils cost five cents each and a ream of paper costs $7.50, how much does it cost to supply the office for a week?
   a. $7.55
   b. $12.20
   c. $27.45
   d. $38.25

▶ Part 2: Word Knowledge

Time: 11 minutes

Select the choice that best matches the underlined word.

1. Mediate most nearly means
   a. ponder.
   b. interfere.
   c. reconcile.
   d. dissolve.

2. The attorney wanted to expedite the process.
   a. accelerate
   b. evaluate
   c. reverse
   d. justify

3. The student gave a plausible explanation for his lateness so it was excused by the teacher.
   a. unbelievable
   b. credible
   c. insufficient
   d. apologetic

4. Concurrent most nearly means
   a. incidental.
   b. simultaneous.
   c. apprehensive.
   d. substantial.

5. Impromptu most nearly means
   a. tactless.
   b. passive.
   c. rehearsed.
   d. spontaneous.

6. Induce most nearly means
   a. prompt.
   b. withdraw.
   c. presume.
   d. represent.

7. He based his conclusion on what he inferred from the evidence, not on what he actually observed.
   a. intuited
   b. imagined
   c. surmised
   d. implied

8. Saturate most nearly means
   a. deprive.
   b. construe.
   c. soak.
   d. verify.

9. Synopsis most nearly means
   a. summary.
   b. abundance.
   c. stereotype.
   d. verify.

10. Hyperbole most nearly means
   a. sincerity.
   b. exaggeration.
   c. understatement.
   d. indignation.

11. Proscribe most nearly means
   a. measure.
   b. recommend.
   c. detect.
   d. forbid.

12. Proponent most nearly means
   a. advocate.
   b. delinquent.
   c. idealist.
   d. critic.

13. Intrepid most nearly means
   a. belligerent.
   b. consistent.
   c. timid.
   d. fearless.

14. Statute most nearly means
   a. replica.
   b. ordinance.
   c. collection.
   d. hypothesis.

15. The general public was apathetic about the verdict.
   a. enraged
   b. indifferent
   c. suspicious
   d. saddened

16. The theories of some astronomers were fortified by the new research.
   a. reinforced
   b. altered
   c. disputed
   d. developed

17. Refrain most nearly means
   a. desist.
   b. secure.
   c. glimpse.
   d. persevere.

18. One of the duties of a captain is to delegate responsibility.
   a. analyze
   b. respect
   c. criticize
   d. assign

19. Spurious most nearly means
   a. prevalent.
   b. false.
   c. melancholy.
   d. actual.

20. The spokesperson must articulate the philosophy of an entire department.
   a. trust
   b. refine
   c. verify
   d. express

21. <u>Disparage</u> most nearly means
a. endorse.
b. finalize.
c. restrict.
d. criticize.

22. The hospital was an <u>expansive</u> facility.
a. obsolete
b. meager
c. spacious
d. costly

23. <u>Urbane</u> most nearly means
a. foolish.
b. vulgar.
c. sophisticated.
d. sentimental.

24. <u>Rationale</u> most nearly means
a. explanation.
b. regret.
c. denial.
d. anticipation.

25. The ruling proved to be <u>detrimental</u> to the investigation.
a. decisive
b. harmful
c. worthless
d. advantageous

► Part 3: Paragraph Comprehension

Time: 13 minutes

Read the passages and answer the questions that follow.

Hearsay evidence, which is the secondhand reporting of a statement, is allowed in court only when the truth of the statement is irrelevant. Hearsay that depends on the statement's truthfulness is inadmissible because the witness does not appear in court and swear an oath to tell the truth. Because his or her demeanor when making the statement is not visible to the jury, the accuracy of the statement cannot be tested under cross-examination, and to introduce it would be to deprive the accused of the constitutional right to confront the accuser. Hearsay is admissible, however, when the truth of the statement is unimportant. If, for example, a defendant claims to have been unconscious at a certain time, and a witness claims that the defendant actually spoke to her at that time, this evidence would be admissible because the truth of what the defendant actually said is irrelevant.

1. The main purpose of the passage is to
a. explain why hearsay evidence abridges the rights of the accused.
b. question the probable truthfulness of hearsay evidence.
c. argue that rules about the admissibility of hearsay evidence should be changed.
d. specify which use of hearsay evidence is inadmissible and why.

2. Which of the following is NOT a reason given in the passage for the inadmissibility of hearsay evidence?
   a. Rumors are not necessarily credible.
   b. The person making the original statement was not under oath.
   c. The jury should be able to watch the gestures and facial expressions of the person making the statement.
   d. The person making the statement cannot be cross-examined.

3. How does the passage explain the proper use of hearsay evidence?
   a. by listing a set of criteria
   b. by providing a hypothetical example
   c. by referring to the Constitution
   d. by citing case law

4. The passage suggests that the criterion used for deciding that most hearsay evidence is inadmissible was most likely
   a. the unreliability of most hearsay witnesses.
   b. the importance of physical evidence to corroborate witness testimony.
   c. concern for discerning the truth in a fair manner.
   d. doubt about the relevance of hearsay testimony.

During the next ten months, all bus operators with two or more years of service will be required to have completed twenty hours of refresher training on one of the Vehicle Maneuvering Training Buses.

Instructors who have used this new technology report that trainees develop skills more quickly than with traditional training methods. In refresher training, this new system reinforces defensive driving skills and safe driving habits. Drivers can also check their reaction times and hand-eye coordination.

5. All bus operators are required to do which of the following?
   a. receive training in defensive driving and operating a computer
   b. complete ten months of refresher driver training
   c. train new drivers on how to operate a simulator
   d. complete twenty hours of training on a simulator

6. The main purpose of the refresher training course on the simulator is to
   a. make sure that all bus operators are maintaining proper driving habits.
   b. give experienced bus operators an opportunity to learn new driving techniques.
   c. help all bus operators to develop hand-eye coordination.
   d. reduce the city's operating budget.

The city has distributed standardized recycling containers to all households with directions that read: "We would prefer that you use this new container as your primary recycling container. Additional recycling containers may be purchased from the city."

7. According to the directions, each household
   a. may only use one recycling container.
   b. must use the new recycling container.
   c. should use the new recycling container.
   d. must buy a new recycling container.

8. According to the directions, which of the following is true about the new containers?
   a. The new containers are better than other containers.
   b. Households may use only the new containers for recyclable items.
   c. The new containers hold more than the old containers did.
   d. Households may use other containers besides the new ones if they wish.

After a snow or ice fall, the city streets are treated with ordinary rock salt. In some areas, the salt is combined with calcium chloride, which is more effective in below-zero temperatures and which melts ice better. This combination of salt and calcium chloride is also less damaging to foliage along the roadways.

9. In deciding whether to use ordinary rock salt or the salt and calcium chloride on a particular street, which of the following is NOT a consideration?
   a. the temperature at the time of treatment
   b. the plants and trees along the street
   c. whether there is ice on the street
   d. whether the street is a main or secondary road

10. According to the snow treatment directions, which of the following is true?
   a. If the temperature is below zero, salt and calcium chloride is effective in treating snow- and ice-covered streets.
   b. Crews must wait until the snow or ice stops falling before salting streets.
   c. The city always salts major roads first.
   d. If the snowfall is light, the city will not salt the streets as this would be a waste of the salt supply.

On February 3, 1956, Autherine Lucy became the first African-American student to attend the University of Alabama, although the dean of women refused to allow Autherine to live in a university dormitory. White students rioted in protest of her admission, and the federal government had to assume command of the Alabama National Guard in order to protect her. Nonetheless, on her first day in class, Autherine bravely took a seat in the front row. She remembers being surprised that the professor of the class appeared not to notice she was even in class. Later she would appreciate his seeming indifference, as he was one of only a few professors to speak out in favor of her right to attend the university.

11. This passage is most likely from a book called
   a. *Twentieth Century United States History.*
   b. *A Collection of Favorite Children's Stories.*
   c. *A History of the Civil War.*
   d. *How to Choose the College That Is Right for You.*

12. According to the passage, Autherine Lucy
   a. lived in a dormitory.
   b. sat in the front row of her class.
   c. became a lawyer.
   d. majored in history.

Detectives who routinely investigate violent crimes can't help but become somewhat jaded. Paradoxically, the victims and witnesses with whom they work closely are often in a highly vulnerable and emotional state. The emotional fallout from a sexual assault, for example, can be complex and long-lasting. Detectives must be trained to handle people in emotional distress and must be sensitive to the fact that for the victim the crime is not routine. At the same time, detectives must recognize the limits of their role and resist the temptation to act as therapists or social workers, instead referring victims to the proper agencies.

13. What is the main idea of the passage?
   a. Detectives who investigate violent crime must not become emotionally hardened by the experience.
   b. Victims of violent crime should be referred to therapists and social workers.
   c. Detectives should be sensitive to the emotional state of victims of violent crime.
   d. Detectives should be particularly careful in dealing with victims of sexual assault.

14. According to the passage, what is "paradoxical" about the detective's relationship to the victim?
- **a.** Detectives know less about the experience of violent crime than do victims.
- **b.** What for the detective is routine is a unique and profound experience for the victim.
- **c.** Detectives must be sensitive to victims' needs, but can't be social workers or psychologists.
- **d.** Not only must detectives solve crimes, but they must also handle the victims with care.

15. Which of the following is NOT advocated by the passage for detectives who investigate violent crimes?
- **a.** They should refer victims to appropriate support services.
- **b.** They should be aware of the psychological consequences of being victimized.
- **c.** They should not become jaded.
- **d.** They should not become too personally involved with victims' problems.

▶ Part 4: Mathematics Knowledge

Time: 24 minutes

1. In the figure below, angle *POS* measures 90°. What is the measure of angle *ROQ*?

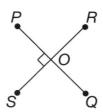

- **a.** 45°
- **b.** 90°
- **c.** 180°
- **d.** 270°

2. $4\frac{1}{5} + 1\frac{2}{5} + 3\frac{3}{10} =$
- **a.** $8\frac{9}{10}$
- **b.** $9\frac{1}{10}$
- **c.** $8\frac{4}{5}$
- **d.** $8\frac{6}{15}$

3. $\frac{3}{4}$ is equal to
- **a.** 0.50.
- **b.** 0.25.
- **c.** 0.75.
- **d.** 0.30.

4. $76\frac{1}{2} + 11\frac{5}{6} =$
- **a.** $87\frac{1}{2}$
- **b.** $88\frac{1}{3}$
- **c.** $88\frac{2}{3}$
- **d.** $88\frac{5}{6}$

5. What is the decimal equivalent of $\frac{1}{3}$, rounded to the nearest hundredth?
- **a.** 0.13
- **b.** 0.33
- **c.** 0.50
- **d.** 0.67

6. $\frac{1}{6} + \frac{7}{12} + \frac{2}{3} =$
- **a.** $\frac{10}{24}$
- **b.** $2\frac{1}{6}$
- **c.** $1\frac{5}{6}$
- **d.** $1\frac{5}{12}$

7. What is another name for 20,706?
- **a.** $200 + 70 + 6$
- **b.** $2,000 + 700 + 6$
- **c.** $20,000 + 70 + 6$
- **d.** $20,000 + 700 + 6$

8. What are the missing integers on this number line?

      –5   ☐   0   ☐

    a. –4 and 1
    b. –6 and 1
    c. –6 and –1
    d. 4 and 9

9. $1\frac{1}{2}$ is equal to
    a. 0.50.
    b. 1.25.
    c. 2.50.
    d. 1.50.

10. If $\frac{x}{54} = \frac{2}{9}$, then x is
    a. 12.
    b. 14.
    c. 18.
    d. 108.

11. Which of these is divisible by 6 and 7?
    a. 63
    b. 74
    c. 96
    d. 84

12. What is $\frac{3}{8}$ equal to?
    a. 0.25
    b. 0.333
    c. 0.60
    d. 0.375

13. What is another way to write $4 \times 4 \times 4$?
    a. 3×4
    b. 8×4
    c. 4^3
    d. 3^4

14. Which of the following choices completes this number sentence?
$$5 \underline{\hspace{1cm}} = (10 \times 2) + (5 \times 3)$$
    a. $\times (5 + 2)$
    b. $+ (5 + 2)$
    c. $\times (5 \times 2)$
    d. $+ (5 \times 2)$

15. Which of these is equivalent to 35° C?
$(F = \frac{9}{5}C + 32)$
    a. 105° F
    b. 95° F
    c. 63° F
    d. 19° F

16. What is the volume of a pyramid that has a rectangular base 5 feet by 3 feet and a height of 8 feet? $(V = \frac{1}{3}lwh)$
    a. 16 feet^3
    b. 30 feet^3
    c. 40 feet^3
    d. 120 feet^3

17. What is another way to write 7.25×10^3?
    a. 72.5
    b. 725
    c. 7,250
    d. 72,500

18. How many inches are there in $3\frac{1}{3}$ yards?
    a. 126
    b. 120
    c. 160
    d. 168

19. $\frac{3}{5} =$
    a. 0.60
    b. 0.20
    c. 0.50
    d. 0.80

20. 0.97 is equal to
   a. 97%
   b. 9.7%
   c. 0.97%
   d. 0.097%

21. In a triangle, $\angle A$ is 70° and $\angle B$ is 30°. What is the measure of $\angle C$?
   a. 90°
   b. 70°
   c. 80°
   d. 100°

22. Which value of x will make the following number sentence true?
$$x + 25 = 13$$
   a. −13
   b. −11
   c. −12
   d. 38

23. What is $\frac{1}{10}$ in decimal form?
   a. 0.05
   b. 0.20
   c. 0.10
   d. 0.25

24. How many faces does a cube have?
   a. 4
   b. 6
   c. 8
   d. 12

25. $-\frac{1}{2} =$
   a. −0.50
   b. −1.00
   c. −0.25
   d. 0.50

26. What is the length of a rectangle if its width is 9 feet and its area is 117 square feet?
   a. 1.3 feet
   b. 10.5 feet
   c. 12 feet
   d. 13 feet

27. A square is a special case of all of the following geometric figures EXCEPT a
   a. parallelogram.
   b. rectangle.
   c. rhombus.
   d. trapezoid.

28. What is the value of x in the figure below?

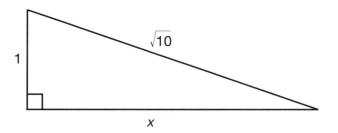

   a. 2
   b. 3
   c. 5
   d. 9

29. $3\frac{1}{4} =$
   a. 3.75
   b. 0.75
   c. 3.5
   d. 3.25

30. If the figure below is a regular decagon with a center at Q, what is the measure of the indicated angle?

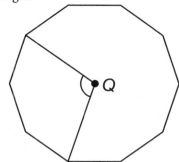

  a. 36°
  b. 45°
  c. 90°
  d. 108°

31. The figure below contains both a circle and a square. What is the area of the entire shaded figure?

  a. $16 + 4\pi$
  b. $16 + 16\pi$
  c. $24 + 2\pi$
  d. $24 + 4\pi$

32. Negative 1.5 is equal to

  a. $1\frac{1}{2}$.
  b. $-1\frac{1}{5}$.
  c. $-\frac{2}{5}$.
  d. $-1\frac{1}{2}$.

33. 62.5% is equal to

  a. $\frac{1}{16}$.
  b. $\frac{5}{8}$.
  c. $6\frac{1}{4}$.
  d. $6\frac{2}{5}$.

34. A line intersects two parallel lines in the figure below. If $\angle P$ measures 40°, what is the measure of $\angle Q$?

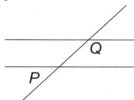

  a. 50°
  b. 60°
  c. 80°
  d. 140°

35. 0.05 is equal to

  a. $\frac{1}{20}$.
  b. $\frac{1}{5}$.
  c. $\frac{1}{10}$.
  d. $\frac{1}{2}$.

▶ Answers

Part 1: Arithmetic Reasoning

1. c. Since the price per copy is $0.75, divide 60 by 0.75 to find the total number that can be purchased with 60; $\frac{60}{0.75} = 80$. Eighty copies can be purchased.

2. c. The volume of the aquarium can be found by using the formula $V = l \times w \times h$. Since the length is 12 inches, the width is 5 inches, and the height is 10 inches, multiply $V = 12 \times 5 \times 10$ to get a volume of 600 cubic inches.

3. c. The value of the handbag ($150) must be included in the total.

4. d. Both choices **a** and **b** can be ruled out because there is no way to determine how many tickets are for adults or for children. Choice **c** can be ruled out because the price of group tickets is not given.

5. d. Because the 15 year old requires an adult ticket, there are three adult tickets at $7.50 each and one child's ticket at $5.

6. a. The adult price on Saturday afternoon is $5.50; the child's price is $3.00.

7. d. This problem is solved by dividing 60 by 0.75.

8. b. This is a simple multiplication problem that is solved by multiplying 35 times 8.2.

9. a. You know the ratio of Drake's charge to Jean's charge is 3 to 4, or $\frac{3}{4}$. To find what Jean charges, you use the equation $\frac{3}{4} = \frac{36}{x}$, or $3x = 4(36)$; $(4)(36) = 144$, which is then divided by 3 to arrive at $x = 48$.

10. a. In this question, you need to find 15% of the 30% of students that are in the music program. To find 15% of 30%, change the percents to decimal form and multiply. Since $30\% = 0.30$ and $15\% = 0.15$, multiply $(0.30)(0.15) = 0.045$. As a decimal, this is equivalent to 4.5% which is choice **a**.

11. d. The basic cable service fee of $15 is 75% of $20.

12. a. The labor fee ($25) plus the deposit ($65) plus the basic service ($15) equals $105. The difference between the total bill, $112.50, and $105 is $7.50, the cost of the news channels.

13. d. Eighty out of 100 is 80%. Eighty percent of 30,000 is 24,000.

14. d. 27.5% of 400 is 110.

15. b. Rock is 45.5%; when we add 4.5% for classical the total is 50%.

16. c. If 60% of the people were satisfied with their new car, 40% were unsatisfied; 40% of 220 is 88.

17. c. Divide 135 Spanish-speaking students by 1,125 total number of students to arrive at .12 or 12%.

18. a. The first step in solving the problem is to subtract 86 from 148. The remainder, 62, is then divided by 2.

19. c. Three feet 4 inches equals 40 inches; 40 divided by 5 is 8.

20. a. It will cost $3 for a sandwich and a cookie. To get two additional sandwiches, it would cost another $4. Therefore, it would cost $7 to get three sandwiches and a cookie. Since she only has $6 to spend, this combination is not possible.

21. d. Area is width times length, in this case, 5 times 7, or 35 square feet.

22. b. Use the formula beginning with the operation in parentheses: $98 - 32 = 66$. Then multiply 66 by $\frac{5}{9}$, first multiplying 66 by 5 to get 330; 330 divided by 9 is 36.66667, which is rounded up to 36.7.

23. c. Each 9-foot wall has an area of 9×8 or 72 square feet. There are two such walls, so those two walls combined have an area of 72×2 or 144 square feet. Each 11-foot wall has an area of 11×8 or 88 square feet, and again there are two such walls: $88 \times 2 = 176$. To find the total surface area, add 144 and 176 to get 320 square feet.

24. b. $1\frac{1}{2}$ cups equals $\frac{3}{2}$ cups. The ratio is 6 people to 4 people, which is equal to the ratio of x to $\frac{3}{2}$. By cross multiplying, we get $6(\frac{3}{2})$ equals $4x$, or 9 equals $4x$. Dividing both sides by 4, we get $\frac{9}{4}$, or $2\frac{1}{4}$ cups.

25. a. The distance between Plattville and Quincy is the hypotenuse of a right triangle with sides of length 80 and 60. The length of the hypotenuse equals the square root of (80^2 + 60^2), which equals the square root of (6,400 + 3,600), which equals the square root of 10,000, which equals 100 miles.

26. d. The volume of concrete is 27 cubic feet. Volume is length times width times depth, or $(l)(w)(d)$, so $(l)(w)(d) = 27$. We're told that the length l is 6 times the width w, so l equals $6w$. We're also told that the depth is 6 inches, or 0.5 feet. Substituting what we know about the length and depth into the original equation and solving for w, we get $(l)(w)(d) = (6w)(w)(0.5) = 27.3w^2 = 27$; $w^2 = 9$, so $w = 3$. To get the length, we remember that l equals $6w$, so l equals $(6)(3)$, or 18 feet.

27. c. Find the price per ounce of each brand, as follows: Brand W is $\frac{21}{6}$ or 3.5 cents per ounce; Brand X is $\frac{48}{15}$ or 3.2 cents per ounce; Brand Y is $\frac{56}{20}$ or 2.8 cents per ounce; Brand Z is $\frac{96}{32}$ or 3.0 cents per ounce. It is then easy to see that Brand Y, at 2.8 cents per ounce, is the least expensive.

28. a. 2,052 miles divided by 6 days is 342 miles per day; 342 miles divided by 2 stops is 171 miles.

29. b. $K + F + S = 540$. Also, $K = 2F$ and $S = 2F$, which changes the original equation to $2F + F + 2F = 540$, so $5F = 540$ and $F = 108$. Since there is one fork per place setting, the cook can buy 108 place settings.

30. c. First find the total price of the pencils: (24 pencils)($0.05) = $1.20. Then find the total price of the paper: (3.5 reams)($7.50 per ream) = $26.25. Next, add the two totals together: $1.20 + 26.25 = $27.45.

Part 2: Word Knowledge

1. c. To *mediate* is to settle disputes; to *reconcile* is to bring into agreement.

2. a. To *expedite* a process is to hurry it up or *accelerate* it.

3. b. If something is *plausible*, it is believable or *credible*.

4. b. *Concurrent* means happening at the same time; *simultaneous* means the same thing.

5. d. *Impromptu* means without preparation; *spontaneous* means unpremeditated.

6. a. To *induce* is to bring about; to *prompt* is to provoke or induce to action.

7. c. To *infer* something is to *surmise* it or deduce it from the evidence.

8. c. To *saturate* is to fill or to load to capacity; to *soak* is to permeate.

9. a. A *synopsis* is an abbreviated version; a *summary* is a brief statement of facts or points.

10. b. A *hyperbole* is an extravagant statement; an *exaggeration* is an overstatement.

11. d. One of the meanings of to *proscribe* is to prohibit; to *forbid* is to command (someone) not to do something. *Proscribe* should not be confused with *prescribe,* which is what a doctor does with a medication.

12. a. A *proponent* is a supporter of something; an *advocate* is someone who supports something—for instance, a cause.

13. d. An *intrepid* person approaches a challenge without fear; a *fearless* person behaves the same way.

14. b. A *statute* is a law; an *ordinance* is a rule or law.

15. b. To be *apathetic* is to show little or no interest, or to be *indifferent*.

16. a. To be *fortified* is to be strengthened or *reinforced*.

17. a. To *refrain* is to hold back from doing something; to *desist* is to cease doing something.

18. d. To *delegate* a task is to *assign* it or to appoint another to do it.

19. **b.** Something that is *spurious* is not genuine; something that is *false* is also not genuine.

20. **d.** To *articulate* something is to give words to it or *express* it.

21. **d.** To *disparage* is to talk about something or someone in a negative manner; to *criticize* is to find fault with.

22. **c.** If something is *expansive*, it is broad, open, or *spacious*.

23. **c.** To be *urbane* is to show the refined manners of high society; to be *sophisticated* is to show worldly knowledge or refinement.

24. **a.** A *rationale* is a reason for something; an *explanation* is a clarification or definition or something.

25. **b.** If a thing is *detrimental*, it is injurious or *harmful*.

Part 3: Paragraph Comprehension

1. **d.** Although the last sentence expands on the main point, the rest of the passage explains why hearsay evidence is only admissible when it doesn't matter whether or not the statement is true.

2. **a.** This statement may be true, but it isn't in the passage.

3. **b.** See the last sentence of the passage.

4. **c.** The passage mentions the truthfulness of testimony several times.

5. **d.** The first two sentences of the passage state that bus operators must have twenty hours of training on a simulator.

6. **a.** The second sentence in the second paragraph states that the simulator reinforces safe driving habits. Although choices **b**, **c**, and **d** are possible benefits of the program, these are not the main purpose of the refresher course.

7. **c.** The directions indicate that the city prefers, but does not require, use of the new container. In addition, it appears the city only charges residents for additional containers.

8. **d.** The directions state the city would like households to use the new containers as their primary containers; this means other containers are allowed.

9. **d.** The directions mention nothing about main or secondary roads.

10. **a.** The other choices are not mentioned in the directions.

11. **a.** The passage states that the events it described happened in 1956; this rules out choice **c**. The purpose of the passage is to explain a historical event, so choices **b** and **d** are clearly wrong.

12. **b.** See the first paragraph. Choice **a** is contradicted in the first paragraph, and the passage does not discuss Lucy's later profession (choice **c**) or major (choice **d**).

13. **c.** Choice **a** is incorrect because the first sentence suggests that becoming hardened is unavoidable. Choices **b** and **d** are implied in the passage but neither is the main idea.

14. **b.** See the first two sentences of the passage.

15. **c.** The passage claims that becoming jaded is inevitable.

Part 4: Mathematics Knowledge

1. **b.** $\overline{PQ}$ and $\overline{RS}$ are intersecting lines. The fact that $\angle POS$ is a 90-degree angle means that $\overline{PQ}$ and $\overline{RS}$ are perpendicular, indicating that all the angles formed by their intersection, including $\angle ROQ$, measure 90°.

2. **a.** Incorrect answers include adding both the numerator and the denominator and not converting fifths to tenths properly.

3. **c.** To convert a fraction to a decimal, divide the numerator, 3, by the denominator, 4; $3.00 \div 4 = 0.75$.

4. **b.** The correct answer is $88\frac{1}{3}$.

5. **b.** Divide the numerator by the denominator; $1.000 \div 3 = 0.33\overline{3}$. Round the answer to the hundredths place (two decimal places) to get the answer 0.33.

6. d. You have to convert all three fractions to twelfths before adding them.

7. d. Choice **a** reads 276; choice **b** reads 2,706; choice **c** reads 20,076.

8. a. The first box is one greater than −5; the second is one greater than 0.

9. d. $1\frac{1}{2}$ is a mixed number. To convert this into a decimal, first take the whole number (in this case, 1) and place it to the left of the decimal point. Then, take the fraction (in this case, $\frac{1}{2}$) and convert it to a decimal by dividing the numerator by the denominator. Putting these two steps together gives the answer, 1.50.

10. a. Raise the fraction $\frac{2}{9}$ to 54ths by multiplying both numerator and denominator by 6.

11. d. $84 \div 6 = 14$; $84 \div 7 = 12$.

12. d. Divide 3 by 8 in order to convert the fraction into a decimal; $3.000 \div 8 = 0.375$.

13. c. The meaning of 4^3 is 4 times itself 3 times.

14. a. The total on the right is 35. On the left, you need an operation you can do on 5 to get 35. Multiplying by 7—5 + 2—does the trick.

15. b. Use 35 for C; $F = (\frac{9}{5} \times 35) + 32$. Therefore $F = 63 + 32$, or 95°.

16. c. $5(3)(8) = 120$; $120 \div 3 = 40$.

17. c. $10(10)(10) = 1,000$; $1,000(7.25) = 7,250$.

18. b. To solve this problem, you must first convert yards to inches. There are 36 inches in a yard; $36(3\frac{1}{3}) = 120$.

19. a. Divide 3 by 5 to convert from a fraction into a decimal; $3.00 \div 5 = 0.60$.

20. a. 0.97 multiplied by 100 is 97; therefore, the correct answer is 97%.

21. c. The sum of the measure of the angles in a triangle is 180°; $70° + 30° = 100°$; $180° - 100° = 80°$. Therefore, angle C is 80°.

22. c. Since the solution to the problem $x + 25 = 13$ is $x = -12$.

23. c. Divide 1 by 10 to convert the fraction into a decimal; $1.00 \div 10 = 0.10$.

24. b. A cube has four sides, a top, and a bottom, which means that it has six faces.

25. a. Divide 1 by 2 in order to convert the fraction into a decimal; $1.00 \div 2 = 0.50$. Finally, add the negative sign to get −0.50.

26. d. To solve this problem you should use the formula $A = lw$, or $117 = 9l$. Next, you must divide 117 by 9 to find the answer.

27. d. A square is a special case of all of these figures except the trapezoid. A square is a parallelogram because its opposite sides are parallel. A square is a rectangle because it is a quadrilateral with 90-degree angles. A square is a rhombus because it is a parallelogram with all sides equal in length. However, a square is not a trapezoid because a trapezoid has only two sides parallel.

28. b. The Pythagorean theorem states that the square of the length of the hypotenuse of a right triangle is equal to the sum of the squares of the other two sides, so we know that $1^2 + x^2 = (\sqrt{10})^2$, so $1 + x^2 = 10$, so $x^2 = 10 - 1 = 9$, so $x = 3$.

29. d. Separate the mixed number into the whole number plus the fraction; $3\frac{1}{4} = 3.0 + \frac{1}{4}$; divide 1 by 4 to convert the fraction to a decimal; $1.00 \div 4 = 0.25$; $3.0 + 0.25 = 3.25$.

30. d. If the figure is a regular decagon, it can be divided into ten equal sections by lines passing through the center. Two such lines form the indicated angle, which includes three of the ten sections; $\frac{3}{10}$ of 360° = 108°.

31. c. The easiest way to calculate the area is to realize that the shaded figure is made up of half a circle of diameter 4 (radius = $\frac{4}{2}$ = 2) on top of a rectangle that is 4 units wide and 6 units tall. The area of a half circle is $(\frac{1}{2})\pi r^2$, and the area of a rectangle is length times width. So the shaded area equals $(\frac{1}{2})\pi(2)^2 + (4)(6) = 24 + 2\pi$.

32. d. Since there is a number 1 to the left of the decimal, this will be the whole number. The fraction is found by using the number to the right of the decimal. The 5 is in the tenths place, so the fraction is $\frac{5}{10}$, which can be reduced to $\frac{1}{2}$ (divide both the numerator and the denominator by 5). The final mixed number is the whole number (1), plus the fraction ($\frac{1}{2}$). Adding the negative, the answer is $-1\frac{1}{2}$.

33. b. 62.5% is $\frac{62.5}{100}$. You should multiply both the numerator and denominator by 10 to move the decimal point, resulting in $\frac{625}{1,000}$, and then factor both the numerator and denominator to find out how far you can reduce the fraction; $\frac{625}{1,000}$ equals $\frac{(5)(5)(5)(5)}{(5)(5)(5)(8)}$. If you cancel the three 5s that are in both the numerator and denominator, you will get $\frac{5}{8}$.

34. d. A line that intersects two parallel lines forms supplementary angles on either side of it. Supplementary angles are angles whose measures add up to 180°; $180 - 40 = 140$.

35. a. In the decimal, 0.05, the 5 falls in the hundredths place (two places to the right of the decimal). To convert this to a fraction, the 5 is placed over 100 and then reduced; $\frac{5 \div 5}{100 \div 5} = \frac{1}{20}$.

Scoring

Write your raw score (the number you got right) for each test in the blanks below. Then turn to Chapter 3 to find out how to convert these raw scores into the scores the armed services use.

1. Arithmetic Reasoning: _____ right out of 30
2. Word Knowledge: _____ right out of 25
3. Paragraph Comprehension: _____ right out of 15
4. Mathematics Knowledge: _____ right out of 35

Here are the steps you should take, depending on your AFQT score on the first practice test:

- **If your AFQT is below 29,** you need more help in reading and/or math. You should spend plenty of time reviewing the lessons and practice questions found in this book.

- **If your AFQT is 29–31,** be sure to focus on your weakest subjects in the review lessons and practice questions that are found in this book.
- **If your AFQT is above 31,** review the areas that give you trouble, and then take the second practice test in Chapter 12 to make sure you are able to get a passing score again.

Math Review

CHAPTER SUMMARY

This chapter gives you some important tips for dealing with math questions and reviews some of the most commonly tested concepts. If you need to learn or review important math skills, this chapter is for you.

Two subtests of the ASVAB—Arithmetic Reasoning and Mathematics Knowledge—cover math skills. Arithmetic Reasoning is basically math word problems. Mathematics Knowledge tests your knowledge of math concepts, principles, and procedures. You don't have to do a lot of calculation in the Mathematics Knowledge subtest; you need to know basic terminology (like *sum* and *perimeter),* formulas (such as the area of a square), and computation rules. Both subtests cover the subjects you probably studied in school. This chapter reviews concepts you will need for both Arithmetic Reasoning and Mathematics Knowledge. Chapter 7 gives you more of these types of problems for extra practice.

▶ Math Strategies

- **Don't work in your head!** Use your test book or scratch paper to take notes, draw pictures, and calculate. Although you might think that you can solve math questions more quickly in your head, that's a good way to make mistakes. Write out each step.

- **Read a math question in *chunks* rather than straight through from beginning to end.** As you read each *chunk,* stop to think about what it means and make notes or draw a picture to represent that *chunk.*
- **When you get to the actual question, circle it.** This will keep you more focused as you solve the problem.
- **Glance at the answer choices for clues.** If they are fractions, you probably should do your work in fractions; if they are decimals, you should probably work in decimals; etc.
- **Make a plan of attack to help you solve the problem.**
- **If a question stumps you, try one of the *backdoor* approaches explained in the next section.** These are particularly useful for solving word problems.
- **When you get your answer, reread the circled question to make sure you have answered it.** This helps avoid the careless mistake of answering the wrong question.
- **Check your work after you get an answer.** Test-takers get a false sense of security when they get an answer that matches one of the multiple-choice answers. Here are some good ways to check your work *if you have time:*
  - Ask yourself if your answer is reasonable, if it makes sense.
  - Plug your answer back into the problem to make sure the problem holds together.
  - Do the question a second time, but use a different method.
- **Approximate when appropriate.** For example:
  - $5.98 + $8.97 is a little less than $15. (Add: $6 + $9)
  - .9876 × 5.0342 is close to 5. (Multiply: $1 × 5$)
- **Skip hard questions and come back to them later.** Mark them in your test book so you can find them quickly.

Backdoor Approaches for Answering Tough Questions

Many word problems are actually easier to solve by backdoor approaches. The two techniques that follow are time-saving ways to solve multiple-choice word problems that you don't know how to solve with a straightforward approach. The first technique, *nice numbers*, is useful when there are unknowns (like *x*) in the text of the word problem, making the problem too abstract for you. The second technique, *working backward*, presents a quick way to substitute numeric answer choices back into the problem to see which one works.

Nice Numbers

1. When a question contains unknowns, like *x*, plug nice numbers in for the unknowns. A nice number is easy to calculate with and makes sense in the problem.
2. Read the question with the nice numbers in place. Then solve it.
3. If the answer choices are all numbers, the choice that matches your answer is the right one.
4. If the answer choices contain unknowns, substitute the same nice numbers into all the answer choices. The choice that matches your answer is the right one. If more than one answer matches, do the problem again with different nice numbers. You will only have to check the answer choices that have already matched.

Example:

Judi went shopping with *p* dollars in her pocket. If the price of shirts was *s* shirts for *d* dollars, what is the maximum number of shirts Judi could buy with the money in her pocket?

a. *psd*

b. $\frac{ps}{d}$

c. $\frac{pd}{s}$

d. $\frac{ds}{p}$

To solve this problem, let's try these nice numbers: $p = \$100$, $s = 2$; $d = \$25$. Now reread it with the numbers in place:

> Judi went shopping with *$100* in her pocket. If the price of shirts was *2* shirts for *$25*, what is the maximum number of shirts Judi could buy with the money in her pocket?

Since 2 shirts cost $25, that means that 4 shirts cost $50, and 8 shirts cost $100. So our answer is 8. Let's substitute the nice numbers into all 4 answers:

a. $100 \times 2 \times 25 = 5,000$

b. $\frac{100 \times 2}{25} = 8$

c. $\frac{100 \times 25}{2} = 1,250$

d. $\frac{25 \times 2}{100} = \frac{1}{2}$

The answer is **b** because it is the only one that matches our answer of 8.

Working Backward

You can frequently solve a word problem by plugging the answer choices back into the text of the problem to see which one fits all the facts stated in the problem. The process is faster than you think because you will probably only have to substitute one or two answers to find the right one.

This approach works only when:

- All of the answer choices are numbers.
- You are asked to find a simple number, not a sum, product, difference, or ratio.

Here's What to Do

1. Look at all the answer choices and begin with the one in the middle of the range. For example, if the answers are 14, 8, 2, 20, and 25, begin by plugging 14 into the problem.
2. If your choice doesn't work, eliminate it. Determine if you need a bigger or smaller answer.
3. Plug in one of the remaining choices.
4. If none of the answers works, you may have made a careless error. Begin again or look for your mistake.

Example:

> Juan ate $\frac{1}{3}$ of the jellybeans. Maria then ate $\frac{3}{4}$ of the remaining jellybeans, which left 10 jellybeans. How many jellybeans were there to begin with?
> **a.** 60
> **b.** 80
> **c.** 90
> **d.** 120

Starting with the middle answer, let's assume there were 90 jellybeans to begin with:

> Since Juan ate $\frac{1}{3}$ of them, that means he ate 30 ($\frac{1}{3} \times 90 = 30$), leaving 60 of them ($90 - 30 = 60$). Maria then ate $\frac{3}{4}$ of the 60 jellybeans, or 45 of them ($\frac{3}{4} \times 60 = 45$). That leaves 15 jellybeans ($60 - 45 = 15$).

The problem states that there were 10 jellybeans left, and we wound up with 15 of them. That indicates that we started with too big a number. Thus, 90 and 120 are incorrect! With only two choices left, let's use common sense to decide which one to try. The next lower answer is only a little smaller than 90 and may not be small enough. So, let's try 60:

> Since Juan ate $\frac{1}{3}$ of them, that means he ate 20 ($\frac{1}{3} \times 60 = 20$), leaving 40 of them ($60 - 20 = 40$). Maria then ate $\frac{3}{4}$ of the 40 jellybeans, or 30 of them ($\frac{3}{4} \times 40 = 30$). That leaves 10 jellybeans ($40 - 30 = 10$).

Because this result of 10 jellybeans remaining agrees with the problem, the correct answer is **a.**

Glossary of Terms

Denominator   the bottom number in a fraction. *Example:* 2 is the denominator in $\frac{1}{2}$.

Difference   subtract. The difference of 2 numbers means subtract one number from the other.

Divisible by   a number is divisible by a second number if that second number divides *evenly* into the original number. *Example:* 10 is divisible by 5 ($10 \div 5 = 2$, with no remainder). However, 10 is not divisible by 3. (See *multiple of*)

Even Integer   integers that are divisible by 2, like . . . –4, –2, 0, 2, 4. . . . *(See integer)*

Integer   numbers along the number line, like . . . –3, –2, –1, 0, 1, 2, 3. . . . Integers include the whole numbers and their opposites. (See *whole number*)

Multiple of   a number is a multiple of a second number if that second number can be multiplied by an integer to get the original number. *Example:* 10 is a multiple of 5 ($10 = 5 \times 2$); however, 10 is not a multiple of 3. (See *divisible by*)

Negative Number a number that is less than zero, like . . . –1, –18.6, $-\frac{3}{4}$. . . .

Numerator   the top part of a fraction. *Example:* 1 is the numerator of $\frac{1}{2}$.

Odd Integer   integers that aren't divisible by 2, like . . . –5, –3, –1, 1, 3. . . .

Positive Number a number that is greater than zero, like . . . 2, 42, $\frac{1}{2}$, 4.63. . . .

Prime Number   integers that are divisible only by 1 and themselves, like . . . 2, 3, 5, 7, 11. . . . All prime numbers are odd, except for the number 2. The number 1 is not considered prime.

Product   multiply. The product of two numbers means the numbers are multiplied together.

Quotient   the answer you get when you divide. *Example:* 10 divided by 5 is 2; the quotient is 2.

Real Number   all the numbers you can think of, like . . . 17, –5, $\frac{1}{2}$, –23.6, 3.4329, 0. . . . Real numbers include the integers, fractions, and decimals. (See *integer*)

Remainder   the number left over after division. *Example:* 11 divided by 2 is 5, with a remainder of 1.

Sum   add. The sum of two numbers means the numbers are added together.

Whole Number   numbers you can count on your fingers, like . . . 1, 2, 3. . . . All whole numbers are positive.

▶ Word Problems

Many of the math problems on tests are word problems. A word problem can include any kind of math, including simple arithmetic, fractions, decimals, percentages, even algebra and geometry.

The hardest part of any word problem is translating English into math. When you read a problem, you can frequently translate it *word for word* from English statements into mathematical statements. At other times, however, a key word in the word problem hints at the mathematical operation to be performed. Here are the translation rules:

EQUALS   key words: *is, are, has*

English	Math
Bob is 18 years old.	$b = 18$
There are seven hats.	$h = 7$
Judi has five books.	$j = 5$

ADDITION   key words: *sum; more, greater, or older than; total; altogether*

English	Math
The sum of two numbers is 10.	$x + y = 10$
Karen has $5 more than Sam.	$k = 5 + s$
The base is 3" greater than the height.	$b = 3 + h$
Judi is two years older than Tony.	$j = 2 + t$
The total of three numbers is 25.	$a + b + c = 25$
How much do Joan and Tom have altogether?	$j + t = ?$

SUBTRACTION   key words: *difference, fewer, less or younger than, remain, left over*

English	Math
The difference between two numbers is 17.	$x - y = 17$
Mike has five fewer cats than twice the number Jan has.	$m = 2j - 5$
Jay is two years younger than Brett.	$j = b - 2$
After Carol ate three apples, r apples remained.	$r = a - 3$

MULTIPLICATION   key words: *of, product, times*

English	Math
Twenty percent of Matthew's baseball caps	$0.20 \times m$
Half of the boys	$\frac{1}{2} \times b$
The product of two numbers is 12.	$a \times b = 12$

DIVISION   key word: *per*

English	Math
15 drops per teaspoon	$\frac{15 \text{ drops}}{\text{teaspoon}}$
22 miles per gallon	$\frac{22 \text{ miles}}{\text{gallon}}$

Distance Formula: Distance = Rate x Time

The key words are words that imply movement like: *plane, train, boat, car, walk, run, climb,* or *swim.*

- How far did the plane travel in four hours if it averaged 300 miles per hour?

  $d = 300 \times 4$

  $d = 1{,}200$ miles

- Ben walked 20 miles in four hours. What was his average speed?

  $20 = r \times 4$

  five miles per hour $= r$

Solving a Word Problem Using the Translation Table

Remember the problem at the beginning of this chapter about the jellybeans?

Juan ate $\frac{1}{3}$ of the jellybeans. Maria then ate $\frac{3}{4}$ of the remaining jellybeans, which left 10 jellybeans. How many jellybeans were there to begin with?

a. 60

b. 80

c. 90

d. 120

We solved it by *working backward.* Now let's solve it using our translation rules.

Assume Juan started with J jellybeans. Eating $\frac{1}{3}$ of them means eating $\frac{1}{3} \times J$ jellybeans. Maria ate a fraction of the remaining jellybeans, which means we must subtract to find out how many are left: $J - \frac{1}{3} \times J = \frac{2}{3} \times J$. Maria then ate $\frac{3}{4}$, leaving $\frac{1}{4}$ of the $\frac{2}{3} \times J$ jellybeans, or $\frac{1}{4} \times \frac{2}{3} \times J$ jellybeans. Multiplying out $\frac{1}{4} \times \frac{2}{3} \times J$ gives $\frac{1}{6}J$ as the number of jellybeans left. The problem states that there were 10 jellybeans left, meaning that we set $\frac{1}{6} \times J$ equal to 10: $\frac{1}{6} \times J = 10$.

Solving this equation for J gives $J = 60$. Thus, the right answer is **a** (the same answer we got when we *worked backward*). As you can see, both methods—working backward and translating from English to math—work. You should use whichever method is more comfortable for you.

Practice Word Problems

You will find word problems using fractions, decimals, and percentages in those sections of this chapter. For now, practice using the translation table on problems that just require you to work with basic arithmetic. Answers are found on page 93.

1. Joan went shopping with $100 and returned home with only $18.42. How much money did she spend?
   a. $81.58
   b. $72.68
   c. $72.58
   d. $71.58

2. Mark invited ten friends to a party. Each friend brought three guests. How many people came to the party, excluding Mark?
   a. 3
   b. 10
   c. 30
   d. 40

3. The office secretary can type 80 words per minute on his word processor. How many minutes will it take him to type a report containing 760 words?
   a. 8
   b. $8\frac{1}{2}$
   c. 9
   d. $9\frac{1}{2}$

4. Mr. Wallace is writing a budget request to upgrade his personal computer system. He wants to purchase a cable modem, which will cost $100, two new software programs at $350 each, a color printer for $249, and an additional color cartridge for $25. What is the total amount Mr. Wallace should write on his budget request?
   a. $724
   b. $974
   c. $1,049
   d. $1,074

► Fraction Review

Problems involving fractions may be straightforward calculation questions, or they may be word problems. Typically, they ask you to add, subtract, multiply, divide, or compare fractions.

Working with Fractions

A fraction is a part of something.

> *Example:* Let's say that a pizza was cut into eight equal slices and you ate three of them. The fraction $\frac{3}{8}$ tells you what part of the pizza you ate. The pizza below shows this: Three of the eight pieces (the ones you ate) are shaded.

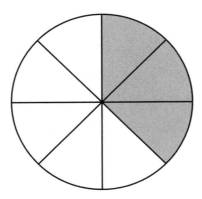

THREE KINDS OF FRACTIONS

Proper fraction	The top number is less than the bottom number: $\frac{1}{2}; \frac{2}{3}; \frac{4}{9}; \frac{8}{13}$ The value of a proper fraction is less than 1.
Improper fraction	The top number is greater than or equal to the bottom number: $\frac{3}{2}; \frac{5}{3}; \frac{14}{9}; \frac{12}{12}$ The value of an improper fraction is 1 or more.
Mixed number	A fraction written to the right of a whole number: $3\frac{1}{2}; 4\frac{2}{3}; 12\frac{3}{4}; 24\frac{3}{4}$ The value of a mixed number is more than 1: it is the sum of the whole number plus the fraction.

Changing Improper Fractions into Mixed or Whole Numbers

It's easier to add and subtract fractions that are mixed numbers rather than improper fractions. To change an improper fraction, say $\frac{13}{2}$, into a mixed number, follow these steps:

1. Divide the bottom number (2) into the top number (13) to get the whole number portion (6) of the mixed number:

$$\begin{array}{r} 6 \\ 2\overline{)13} \\ \underline{12} \\ 1 \end{array}$$

2. Write the remainder of the division (1) over the old bottom number (2): $6\frac{1}{2}$
3. Check: Change the mixed number back into an improper fraction (see steps below).

Changing Mixed Numbers into Improper Fractions

It's easier multiply and divide fractions when you're working with improper fractions rather than mixed numbers. To change a mixed number, say $2\frac{3}{4}$, into an improper fraction, follow these steps:

1. Multiply the whole number (2) by the bottom number (4): $2 \times 4 = 8$
2. Add the result (8) to the top number (3): $8 + 3 = 11$
3. Put the total (11) over the bottom number (4): $\frac{11}{4}$
4. Check: Reverse the process by changing the improper fraction into a mixed number. If you get back the number you started with, your answer is right.

Reducing Fractions

Reducing a fraction means writing it in *lowest terms,* that is, with smaller numbers. For instance, 50¢ is $\frac{50}{100}$ of a dollar, or $\frac{1}{2}$ of a dollar. In fact, if you have 50¢ in your pocket, you say that you have half a dollar. Reducing a fraction does not change its value.

Follow these steps to reduce a fraction:

1. Find a whole number that divides *evenly* into both numbers that make up the fraction.
2. Divide that number into the top of the fraction, and replace the top of the fraction with the quotient (the answer you got when you divided).
3. Do the same thing to the bottom number.
4. Repeat the first three steps until you can't find a number that divides evenly into both numbers of the fraction.

For example, let's reduce $\frac{8}{24}$. We could do it in two steps $\frac{8 \div 4}{24 \div 4} = \frac{2}{6}$; then $\frac{2 \div 2}{6 \div 2} = \frac{1}{3}$. Or we could do it in a single step $\frac{8 \div 8}{24 \div 8} = \frac{1}{3}$.

Shortcut: When the top and bottom numbers both end in zeroes, cross out the same number of zeroes in both numbers to begin the reducing process. For example $\frac{300}{4,000}$ reduces to $\frac{3}{40}$ when you cross out two zeroes in both numbers.

Whenever you do arithmetic with fractions, reduce your answer. On a multiple-choice test, don't panic if your answer isn't listed. Try to reduce it and then compare it to the choices.

Reduce these fractions to lowest terms.

5. $\frac{3}{12} =$

6. $\frac{14}{35} =$

7. $\frac{27}{72} =$

Raising Fractions to Higher Terms

Before you can add and subtract fractions, you have to know how to raise a fraction to higher terms. This is actually the opposite of reducing a fraction.

Follow these steps to raise $\frac{2}{3}$ to 24ths:

1. Divide the old bottom number (3) into the new one (24): $\frac{3}{24} = 8$

2. Multiply the answer (8) by the old top number (2): $2 \times 8 = 16$

3. Put the answer (16) over the new bottom number (24): $\frac{16}{24}$

4. Check: Reduce the new fraction to see if you get back the original one: $\frac{16 \div 8}{24 \div 8} = \frac{2}{3}$

Raise these fractions to higher terms.

8. $\frac{5}{12} = \frac{}{24}$

9. $\frac{2}{9} = \frac{}{27}$

10. $\frac{2}{5} = \frac{}{500}$

Adding Fractions

If the fractions have the same bottom numbers, just add the top numbers together and write the total over the bottom number.

Examples: $\frac{2}{9} + \frac{4}{9} = \frac{6}{9}$ Reduce the sum: $\frac{2}{3}$.

          $\frac{5}{8} + \frac{7}{8} = \frac{12}{8}$ Change the sum to a mixed number: $1\frac{4}{8}$; then reduce: $1\frac{1}{2}$.

There are a few extra steps to add mixed numbers with the same bottom numbers, say $2\frac{3}{5} + 1\frac{4}{5}$:

1. Add the fractions: $\qquad\qquad\qquad\qquad\qquad\qquad$ $\frac{3}{5} + \frac{4}{5} = \frac{7}{5}$

2. Change the improper fraction into a mixed number: $\frac{7}{5} = 1\frac{2}{5}$

3. Add the whole numbers: $\qquad\qquad\qquad\qquad\qquad$ $2 + 1 = 3$

4. Add the results of steps 2 and 3: $\qquad\qquad\qquad$ $1\frac{2}{5} + 3 = 4\frac{2}{5}$

Finding the Least Common Denominator

If the fractions you want to add don't have the same bottom number, you will have to raise some or all of the fractions to higher terms so that they all have the same bottom number, called the **common denominator**. All of the original bottom numbers divide evenly into the common denominator. If it is the smallest number that they all divide evenly into, it is called the **least common denominator (LCD)**.

Here are a few tips for finding the LCD, the smallest number that all the bottom numbers evenly divide into:

- See if all the bottom numbers divide evenly into the biggest bottom number.
- Look at a multiplication table of the largest bottom number until you find a number that all the other bottom numbers evenly divide into.
- When all else fails, multiply all the bottom numbers together.

Example: $\frac{2}{3} + \frac{4}{5}$

1. Find the LCD. Multiply the bottom numbers: $\qquad$ $3 \times 5 \;=\; 15$

2. Raise each fraction to 15ths: $\qquad\qquad\qquad\qquad$ $\frac{2}{3} \;=\; \frac{10}{15}$

$\qquad\qquad\qquad\qquad\qquad\qquad\qquad\qquad\qquad +\frac{4}{5} \;=\; \frac{12}{15}$

$\qquad\qquad\qquad\qquad\qquad\qquad\qquad\qquad\qquad\qquad\quad \overline{\frac{22}{15}}$

3. Add as usual:

Try these addition problems.

11. $\frac{3}{4} + \frac{1}{6} =$

12. $\frac{7}{8} + \frac{2}{3} + \frac{3}{4} =$

13. $4\frac{1}{3} + 2\frac{3}{4} + \frac{1}{6} =$

Subtracting Fractions

If the fractions have the same bottom numbers, just subtract the top numbers and write the difference over the bottom number.

Example: $\frac{4}{9} - \frac{3}{9} = \frac{4-3}{9} = \frac{1}{9}$

If the fractions you want to subtract don't have the same bottom number, you will have to raise some or all of the fractions to higher terms so that they all have the same bottom number, or LCD. If you forgot how to find the LCD, just read the section on adding fractions with different bottom numbers.

Example: $\frac{5}{6} - \frac{3}{4}$

1. Raise each fraction to 12ths because 12 is the LCD, the smallest number that 6 and 4 both divide into evenly:

2. Subtract as usual:

$$\begin{array}{r} \frac{5}{6} = \frac{10}{12} \\ -\frac{3}{4} = \frac{9}{12} \\ \hline \frac{1}{12} \end{array}$$

Subtracting mixed numbers with the same bottom number is similar to adding mixed numbers.

Example: $4\frac{3}{5} - 1\frac{2}{5}$

1. Subtract the fractions: $\qquad\qquad \frac{3}{5} - \frac{2}{5} = \frac{1}{5}$

2. Subtract the whole numbers: $\qquad 4 - 1 = 3$

3. Add the results of steps 1 and 2: $\quad \frac{1}{5} + 3 = 3\frac{1}{5}$

Sometimes there is an extra "borrowing" step when you subtract mixed numbers with the same bottom numbers, say $7\frac{3}{5} - 2\frac{4}{5}$:

1. You can't subtract the fractions the way they are because $\frac{4}{5}$ is bigger than $\frac{3}{5}$. So you borrow 1 from the 7, making it 6, and change that 1 to $\frac{5}{5}$ because 5 is the bottom number: $\qquad 7\frac{3}{5} = 6\frac{5}{5} + \frac{3}{5}$

2. Add the numbers from step 1: $\qquad\qquad\qquad\qquad\qquad 6\frac{5}{5} + \frac{3}{5} = 6\frac{8}{5}$

3. Now you have a different version of the original problem: $\qquad 6\frac{8}{5} - 2\frac{4}{5}$

4. Subtract the fractional parts of the two mixed numbers: $\qquad \frac{8}{5} - \frac{4}{5} = \frac{4}{5}$

5. Subtract the whole number parts of the two mixed numbers: $\qquad 6 - 2 = 4$

6. Add the results of the last 2 steps together: $\qquad\qquad 4 + \frac{4}{5} = 4\frac{4}{5}$

Try these subtraction problems.

14. $\frac{4}{5} - \frac{2}{3} =$

15. $\frac{7}{8} - \frac{1}{4} - \frac{1}{2} =$

16. $4\frac{1}{3} - 2\frac{3}{4} =$

Now let's put what you have learned about adding and subtracting fractions to work in some real-life problems.

17. Manuel drove $3\frac{1}{2}$ miles to work. Then he drove $4\frac{3}{4}$ miles to the store. When he left there, he drove 2 miles to the dry cleaners. Then he drove $3\frac{2}{3}$ miles back to work for a meeting. Finally, he drove $3\frac{1}{2}$ miles home. How many miles did he travel in total?

a. $17\frac{5}{12}$

b. $16\frac{5}{12}$

c. $15\frac{7}{12}$

d. $15\frac{5}{12}$

18. Before leaving the warehouse, a truck driver noted that the mileage gauge registered $4,357\frac{4}{10}$ miles. When he arrived at the delivery location, the mileage gauge then registered $4,400\frac{1}{10}$ miles. How many miles did he drive from the warehouse to the delivery location?

a. $42\frac{3}{10}$

b. $42\frac{7}{10}$

c. $43\frac{7}{10}$

d. $47\frac{2}{10}$

Multiplying Fractions

Multiplying fractions is actually easier than adding them. All you do is multiply the top numbers and then multiply the bottom numbers.

Examples: $\quad \frac{2}{3} \times \frac{5}{7} = \frac{2 \times 5}{3 \times 7} = \frac{10}{21}$

$\qquad\qquad \frac{1}{2} \times \frac{3}{5} \times \frac{7}{4} = \frac{1 \times 3 \times 7}{2 \times 5 \times 4} = \frac{21}{40}$

Sometimes you can *cancel* before multiplying. Canceling is a shortcut that makes the multiplication go faster because you're multiplying with smaller numbers. It's very similar to reducing: If there is a number that divides evenly into a top number and bottom number, do that division before multiplying. If you forget to cancel, you will still get the right answer, but you will have to reduce it.

Example: $\quad \frac{5}{6} \times \frac{9}{20}$

1. Cancel the 6 and the 9 by dividing 3 into both of them: $6 \div 3 = 2$ and $9 \div 3 = 3$. Cross out the 6 and the 9.
2. Cancel the 5 and the 20 by dividing 5 into both of them: $5 \div 5 = 1$ and $20 \div 5 = 4$. Cross out the 5 and the 20.
3. Multiply across the new top numbers and the new bottom numbers: $\frac{1 \times 3}{2 \times 4} = \frac{3}{8}$.

Try these multiplication problems.

19. $\frac{1}{5} \times \frac{2}{3} =$

20. $\frac{2}{3} \times \frac{4}{7} \times \frac{3}{5} =$

21. $\frac{3}{4} \times \frac{8}{9} =$

To multiply a fraction by a whole number, first rewrite the whole number as a fraction with a bottom number of 1.

Example: $5 \times \frac{2}{3} = \frac{5}{1} \times \frac{2}{3} = \frac{10}{3}$
(Optional: Convert $\frac{10}{3}$ to a mixed number: $3\frac{1}{3}$)

To multiply with mixed numbers, it's easier to change them to improper fractions before multiplying.

Example: $4\frac{2}{3} \times 5\frac{1}{2}$

1. Convert $4\frac{2}{3}$ to an improper fraction: $\quad\quad\quad 4\frac{2}{3} = \frac{(4 \times 3 + 2)}{3} = \frac{14}{3}$

2. Convert $5\frac{1}{2}$ to an improper fraction: $\quad\quad\quad 5\frac{1}{2} = \frac{(5 \times 2 + 1)}{2} = \frac{11}{2}$

3. Cancel and multiply the fractions: $\quad\quad\quad \frac{\overset{7}{\cancel{14}}}{3} \cdot \frac{11}{\underset{1}{\cancel{2}}} = \frac{77}{3}$

4. Optional: Convert the improper fraction to a mixed number: $\quad \frac{77}{3} = 25\frac{2}{3}$

Now try these multiplication problems with mixed numbers and whole numbers.

22. $4\frac{1}{3} \times \frac{2}{5} =$

23. $2\frac{1}{2} \times 6 =$

24. $3\frac{3}{4} \times 4\frac{2}{5} =$

Here are a few more real-life problems to test your skills.

25. After driving $\frac{2}{3}$ of the 15 miles to work, Mr. Stone stopped to make a phone call. How many miles had he driven when he made his call?
   a. 5
   b. $7\frac{1}{2}$
   c. 10
   d. 12

26. If Henry worked $\frac{3}{4}$ of a 40-hour week, how many hours did he work?

    a. $7\frac{1}{2}$

    b. 10

    c. 25

    d. 30

27. Technician Chin makes $14.00 an hour. When she works more than 8 hours a day, she gets overtime pay of $1\frac{1}{2}$ times her regular hourly wage for the extra hours. How much did she earn for working 11 hours in one day?

    a. $77

    b. $154

    c. $175

    d. $210

Dividing Fractions

To divide one fraction by a second fraction, invert the second fraction (that is, flip the top and bottom numbers) and then multiply.

    Example: $\frac{1}{2} \div \frac{3}{5}$

1. Invert the second fraction ($\frac{3}{5}$): $\frac{5}{3}$

2. Change the division sign ($\div$) to a multiplication sign ($\times$).

3. Multiply the first fraction by the new second fraction: $\frac{1}{2} \times \frac{5}{3} = \frac{1 \times 5}{2 \times 3} = \frac{5}{6}$

    To divide a fraction by a whole number, first change the whole number to a fraction by putting it over 1. Then follow the division steps above.

    Example: $\frac{3}{5} \div 2 = \frac{3}{5} \div \frac{2}{1} = \frac{3}{5} \times \frac{1}{2} = \frac{3 \times 1}{5 \times 2} = \frac{3}{10}$

    When the division problem has a mixed number, convert it to an improper fraction and then divide as usual.

    Example: $2\frac{3}{4} \div \frac{1}{6}$

1. Convert $2\frac{3}{4}$ to an improper fraction: $\qquad 2\frac{3}{4} = \frac{2 \times 4 + 3}{4} = \frac{11}{4}$

2. Divide $\frac{11}{4}$ by $\frac{1}{6}$: $\qquad \frac{11}{4} \div \frac{1}{6} = \frac{11}{4} \times \frac{6}{1}$

3. Flip $\frac{1}{6}$ to $\frac{6}{1}$ change $\div$ to $\times$, cancel and multiply: $\qquad \frac{11}{\underset{2}{4}} \times \frac{\overset{3}{6}}{1} = \frac{11 \times 3}{2 \times 1} = \frac{33}{2}$

Here are a few division problems to try.

28. $\frac{1}{3} \div \frac{2}{3} =$

29. $2\frac{3}{4} \div \frac{1}{2} =$

30. $\frac{3}{5} \div 3 =$

31. $3\frac{3}{4} \div 2\frac{1}{3} =$

Let's wrap this up with some real-life problems.

32. If four friends evenly split $6\frac{1}{2}$ pounds of candy, how many pounds of candy does each friend get?
    a. $\frac{8}{13}$
    b. $1\frac{5}{8}$
    c. $1\frac{1}{2}$
    d. $1\frac{5}{13}$

33. How many $2\frac{1}{2}$-pound chunks of cheese can be cut from a single 20-pound piece of cheese?
    a. 2
    b. 4
    c. 6
    d. 8

34. Ms. Goldbaum earned $36.75 for working $3\frac{1}{2}$ hours. What was her hourly wage?
    a. $10.00
    b. $10.50
    c. $10.75
    d. $12.00

▶ Decimals

A decimal is a special kind of fraction. You use decimals every day when you deal with money—$10.35 is a decimal that represents 10 dollars and 35 cents. The decimal point separates the dollars from the cents. Because there are 100 cents in one dollar, 1¢ is $\frac{1}{100}$ of a dollar, or $.01.

Each decimal digit to the right of the decimal point has a name:

Examples: $.1 = 1$ tenth $= \frac{1}{10}$
$.02 = 2$ hundredths $= \frac{2}{100}$
$.003 = 3$ thousandths $= \frac{3}{1,000}$
$.0004 = 4$ ten-thousandths $= \frac{4}{10,000}$

When you add zeroes after the rightmost decimal place, you don't change the value of the decimal. For example, 6.17 is the same as all of these:

6.170

6.1700

6.17000000000000000

If there are digits on both sides of the decimal point (like 10.35), the number is called a **mixed decimal**. If there are digits only to the right of the decimal point (like .53), the number is called a **decimal**. A whole number (like 15) is understood to have a decimal point at its right (15.). Thus, 15 is the same as 15.0, 15.00, 15.000, and so on.

Changing Fractions to Decimals

To change a fraction to a decimal, divide the bottom number into the top number after you put a decimal point and a few zeroes on the right of the top number. When you divide, bring the decimal point up into your answer.

Example: Change $\frac{3}{4}$ to a decimal.

1. Add a decimal point and two zeroes to the top number (3):   3.00
2. Divide the bottom number (4) into 3.00:
   Bring the decimal point up into the answer:

$$\begin{array}{r} .75 \\ 4\overline{)3.00} \\ \underline{2\ 8} \\ 20 \\ \underline{20} \\ 0 \end{array}$$

3. The quotient (result of the division) is the answer: .75

Some fractions may require you to add many decimal zeroes in order for the division to come out evenly. In fact, when you convert a fraction like $\frac{2}{3}$ to a decimal, you can keep adding decimal zeroes to the top number forever because the division will never come out evenly. As you divide 3 into 2, you will keep getting 6s:

$$2 \div 3 = .6666666666 \text{ etc.}$$

This is called a **repeating decimal** and it can be written as $.6\overline{6}$ or as $.66\frac{2}{3}$. You can approximate it as .67, .667, .6667, and so on.

Changing Decimals to Fractions

To change a decimal to a fraction, write the digits of the decimal as the top number of a fraction and write the decimal's name as the bottom number of the fraction. Then reduce the fraction, if possible.

Example: .018

1. Write 18 as the top of the fraction: $\underline{18}$
2. Three places to the right of the decimal means *thousandths,* so write 1,000 as the bottom number: $\frac{18}{1,000}$
3. Reduce by dividing 2 into the top and bottom numbers: $\frac{18 \div 2}{1,000 \div 2} = \frac{9}{500}$

Change these decimals or mixed decimals to fractions.

35. .005 =

36. 3.48 =

37. 123.456 =

Comparing Decimals

Because decimals are easier to compare when they have the same number of digits after the decimal point, tack zeroes onto the end of the shorter decimals. Then all you have to do is compare the numbers as if the decimal points weren't there.

Example: Compare .08 and .1.

1. Tack one zero at the end of .1: .10
2. To compare .10 to .08, just compare 10 to 8.
3. Since 10 is larger than 8, .1 is larger than .08.

Adding and Subtracting Decimals

To add or subtract decimals, line them up so their decimal points are aligned. You may want to tack on zeroes at the end of shorter decimals so you can keep all your digits lined up evenly. Remember, if a number doesn't have a decimal point, then put one at the right end of the number.

Example: 1.23 + 57 + .038 =

1. Line up the numbers like this:
2. Add.

$$
\begin{array}{r}
1.230 \\
57.000 \\
+\ .038 \\
\hline
58.268
\end{array}
$$

Example: 1.23 − .038 =

1. Line up the numbers like this:
2. Subtract.

$$
\begin{array}{r}
1.230 \\
-\ .038 \\
\hline
1.192
\end{array}
$$

Try these addition and subtraction problems.

38. .905 + .02 + 3.075 =

39. .005 + 8 + .3 =

40. 3.48 − 2.573 =

41. 123.456 − 122 =

42. A park ranger drove 3.7 miles to the state park. He then walked 1.6 miles around the park to make sure everything was all right. He got back into the car, drove 2.75 miles to check on a broken light and then drove 2 miles back to the ranger station. How many miles did he drive in total?
   a. 8.05
   b. 8.45
   c. 8.8
   d. 10
   e. 10.05

43. The average number of customers at a diner fell from 486.4 per week to 402.5 per week. By how many customers per week did the average fall?
   a. 73.9
   b. 83
   c. 83.1
   d. 83.9
   e. 84.9

Multiplying Decimals
To multiply decimals, ignore the decimal points and just multiply the numbers. Then count the total number of decimal digits (the digits to the *right* of the decimal point) in the numbers you are multiplying. Count off that number of digits in your answer beginning at the right side and put the decimal point to the *left* of those digits.

Example: 215.7 × 2.4

1. Multiply 2,157 times 24:
   2,157
   × 24
   8,628
   4,314
   51,768

2. Because there is a total of two decimal digits in 215.7 and 2.4, count off two places from the right in 51,768, placing the decimal point to the *left* of the last two digits: 517.68

If your answer doesn't have enough digits, tack zeroes on to the left of the answer.

Example: $.03 \times .006$

1. Multiply 3 times 6:	$3 \times 6 = 18$
2. You need five decimal digits in your answer, so tack on three zeroes:	00018
3. Put the decimal point at the front of the number (which is five digits in from the right):	.00018

You can practice multiplying decimals with these.

44. $.05 \times .6 =$

45. $.053 \times 6.4 =$

46. $38.1 \times .0184 =$

47. Joe earns $14.50 per hour. Last week he worked 37.5 hours. How much money did he earn that week?
   a. $518.00
   b. $518.50
   c. $536.50
   d. $543.75

48. Nuts cost $3.50 per pound. Approximately how much will 4.25 pounds of nuts cost?
   a. $12.25
   b. $12.88
   c. $14.50
   d. $14.88

Dividing Decimals

To divide a decimal by a whole number, set up the division $(8\overline{).256})$ and immediately bring the decimal point straight up into the answer $(8\overline{).256})$. Then divide as you would normally divide whole numbers.

Example:
```
        .032
   8).256
        0
       25
       24
       16
       16
        0
```

To divide any number by a decimal, there is an extra step to perform before you can divide. Move the decimal point to the very right of the number you are dividing by, counting the number of places you are moving it. Then move the decimal point the same number of places to the right in the number you are dividing into. In other words, first change the problem to one in which you are dividing by a whole number.

Example: $.06\overline{)1.218}$

1. Because there are two decimal digits in .06, move the decimal point two places to the right in both numbers and move the decimal point straight up into the answer:

   $.06.\overline{)1.21.8}$

2. Divide using the new numbers:

```
       20.3
   6)121.8
      12
       01
       00
       18
       18
        0
```

Under certain conditions, you have to tack on zeroes to the right of the last decimal digit in the number you are dividing into:

- if there aren't enough digits for you to move the decimal point to the right.
- if the answer doesn't come out evenly when you do the division.
- if you are dividing a whole number by a decimal. Then you will have to tack on the decimal point as well as some zeroes.

Try your skills on these division problems.

49. $7 \overline{)9.8} =$

50. $.0004 \overline{).0512} =$

51. $.5 \overline{)28.6} =$

52. $.14 \overline{)196} =$

53. If James Worthington drove his truck 92.4 miles in 2.1 hours, what was his average speed in miles per hour?
  a. 41
  b. 44
  c. 90.3
  d. 94.5

54. Mary Sanders walked a total of 18.6 miles in 4 days. On average, how many miles did she walk each day?
  a. 4.15
  b. 4.60
  c. 4.65
  d. 22.60

▶ Percents

A percent is a special kind of fraction or part of something. The bottom number (the *denominator*) is always 100. For example, 17% is the same as $\frac{17}{100}$. Literally, the word *percent* means *per 100 parts*. The root *cent* means 100: A *century* is 100 years; there are 100 *cents* in a dollar, etc. Thus, 17% means 17 parts out of 100. Because fractions can also be expressed as decimals, 17% is also equivalent to .17, which is 17 hundredths.

You come into contact with percents every day. Sales tax, interest, and discounts are just a few common examples.

If you're shaky on fractions, you may want to review the fraction section again before reading further.

Changing a Decimal to a Percent and Vice Versa

To change a decimal to a percent, move the decimal point two places to the right and tack on a percent sign (%) at the end. If the decimal point moves to the very right of the number, you don't have to write the decimal point. If there aren't enough places to move the decimal point, add zeroes on the right before moving the decimal point.

To change a percent to a decimal, drop off the percent sign and move the decimal point two places to the left. If there aren't enough places to move the decimal point, add zeroes on the left before moving the decimal point.

Try changing these decimals to percents.

55. .45 =

56. .008 =

57. $.16\frac{2}{3}$ =

Now, change these percents to decimals.

58. 12% =

59. $87\frac{1}{2}$% =

60. 250% =

Changing a Fraction to a Percent and Vice Versa

To change a fraction to a percent, there are two techniques. Each is illustrated by changing the fraction $\frac{1}{4}$ to a percent:

Technique 1:   Multiply the fraction by 100%.

Multiply $\frac{1}{4}$ by 100%: $\frac{1}{\overset{}{\underset{1}{4}}} \times \frac{\overset{25}{\cancel{100}}\%}{1} = 25\%$.

Technique 2:   Divide the fraction's bottom number into the top number; then move the decimal point two places to the right and tack on a percent sign (%).

Divide 4 into 1 and move the decimal point two places to the right:

$$4\overline{)1.00}^{.25} \qquad .25 = 25\%$$

To change a percent to a fraction, remove the percent sign and write the number over 100. Then reduce if possible.

Example: Change 4% to a fraction.

1. Remove the % and write the fraction 4 over 100: $\frac{4}{100}$

2. Reduce: $\frac{4 \div 4}{100 \div 4} = \frac{1}{25}$

Here's a more complicated example: Change $16\frac{2}{3}$% to a fraction.

1. Remove the % and write the fraction $16\frac{2}{3}$ over 100: $\frac{16\frac{2}{3}}{100}$

2. Since a fraction means "top number divided by bottom number," rewrite the fraction as a division problem: $16\frac{2}{3} \div 100$

3. Change the mixed number ($16\frac{2}{3}$) to an improper fraction ($\frac{50}{3}$): $\frac{50}{3} \div \frac{100}{1}$

4. Flip the second fraction ($\frac{100}{1}$) and multiply: $\frac{\overset{1}{\cancel{50}}}{3} \times \frac{1}{\underset{2}{\cancel{100}}} = \frac{1}{6}$

Try changing these fractions to percents.

61. $\frac{1}{8} =$

62. $\frac{13}{25} =$

63. $\frac{7}{12} =$

Now change these percents to fractions.

64. 95% =

65. $37\frac{1}{2}\% =$

66. 125% =

Sometimes it is more convenient to work with a percentage as a fraction or a decimal. Rather than have to *calculate* the equivalent fraction or decimal, consider memorizing the equivalence table below. Not only will this increase your efficiency on the math test, but it will also be practical for real-life situations.

CONVERSION TABLE		
Decimal	**%**	**Fraction**
.25	25%	$\frac{1}{4}$
.50	50%	$\frac{1}{2}$
.75	75%	$\frac{3}{4}$
.10	10%	$\frac{1}{10}$
.20	20%	$\frac{1}{5}$
.40	40%	$\frac{2}{5}$
.60	60%	$\frac{3}{5}$
.80	80%	$\frac{4}{5}$
$.33\overline{3}$	$33\frac{1}{3}\%$	$\frac{1}{3}$
$.66\overline{6}$	$66\frac{2}{3}\%$	$\frac{2}{3}$

Percent Word Problems

Word problems involving percents come in three main varieties:

- Find a percent of a whole.
  Example: What is 30% of 40?
- Find what percent one number is of another number.
  Example: 12 is what percent of 40?
- Find the whole when the percent of it is given.
  Example: 12 is 30% of what number?

  While each variety has its own approach, there is a single shortcut formula you can use to solve each of these:

  $\frac{is}{of} = \frac{\%}{100}$

  The *is* is the number that usually follows or is just before the word *is* in the question.

  The *of* is the number that usually follows the word *of* in the question.

  The *%* is the number that is in front of the % or *percent* in the question.

  Or you may think of the shortcut formula as:

  $\frac{part}{whole} = \frac{\%}{100}$

  $part \times 100 = whole \times \%$

  To solve each of the three varieties, let's use the fact that the **cross-products** are equal. The cross-products are the products of the numbers diagonally across from each other. Remembering that *product* means *multiply,* here's how to create the cross-products for the percent shortcut:

  $\frac{part}{whole} = \frac{\%}{100}$

  $part \times 100 = whole \times \%$

  Here's how to use the shortcut with cross-products:

- Find a percent of a whole.
  What is 30% of 40?
  30 is the % and 40 is the *of* number: $\frac{is}{40} = \frac{30}{100}$
  Cross multiply and solve for *is*: $is \times 100 = 40 \times 30$
                                                           $is \times 100 = 1,200$
                                                           12 $\times 100 = 1,200$

  Thus, **12 is** 30% of 40.

- Find what percent one number is of another number.
  12 is what percent of 40?
  12 is the *is* number and 40 is the *of* number: $\frac{12}{40} = \frac{\%}{100}$
  Cross multiply and solve for %: $12 \times 100 = 40 \times \%$
                                                           $1,200 = 40 \times \%$
                                                           $1,200 = 40 \times$ **30**

  Thus, 12 is **30% of** 40.

■ Find the whole when the percent of it is given.

    12 is 30% of what number?

    12 is the *is* number and 30 is the %: $\frac{12}{of} = \frac{30}{100}$

    Cross-multiply and solve for the *of* number: $12 \times 100 = of \times 30$

                                                       $1{,}200 = of \times 30$

                                                       $1{,}200 = \mathbf{40} \times 30$

  Thus 12 is 30% **of 40.**

You can use the same technique to find the percent increase or decrease. The *is* number is the actual increase or decrease, and the *of* number is the original amount.

    Example: If a merchant puts his $20 hats on sale for $15, by what percent does he decrease the selling price?

1. Calculate the decrease, the *is* number: $\$20 - \$15 = \$5$

2. The *of* number is the original amount, $20.

3. Set up the equation and solve for *of* by cross multiplying: $\frac{5}{20} = \frac{\%}{100}$

                                                              $5 \times 100 = 20 \times \%$

                                                              $500 = 20 \times \%$

                                                              $500 = 20 \times 25$

4. Thus, the selling price is decreased by **25%**.

    If the merchant later raises the price of the hats from $15 $\frac{5}{15} = \frac{\%}{100}$

    back to $20, don't be fooled into thinking that the percent $5 \times 100 = 15 \times \%$

    increase is also 25%! It's actually more, because the $500 = 15 \times \%$

    increase amount of $5 is now based on a lower original

      price of only $15: $500 = 15 \times 33\frac{1}{3}$

    Thus, the selling price is increased by **33%**.

    Find a percent of a whole.

67. 1% of 25 =

68. 18.2% of 50 =

69. $37\frac{1}{2}$ of 100 =

70. 125% of 60 =

Find what percent one number is of another number.

71. 10 is what % of 20?

72. 4 is what % of 12?

73. 12 is what % of 4?

Find the whole when the percent of it is given.

74. 15% of what number is 15?

75. $37\frac{1}{2}$% of what number is 3?

76. 200% of what number is 20?

Now try your percent skills on some real-life problems.

77. Last Monday, 20% of 140 staff members was absent. How many employees were absent that day?
   a. 14
   b. 28
   c. 112
   d. 126

78. 40% of Vero's postal service employees are women. If there are 80 women in Vero's postal service, how many men are employed there?
   a. 32
   b. 112
   c. 120
   d. 160

79. Of the 840 shirts sold at a retail store last month, 42 had short sleeves. What percent of the shirts were short sleeved?
   a. .5%
   b. 2%
   c. 5%
   d. 20%

80. Sam's Shoe Store put all of its merchandise on sale for 20% off. If Jason saved $10 by purchasing one pair of shoes during the sale, what was the original price of the shoes before the sale?
   a. $12
   b. $20
   c. $40
   d. $50

▶ Averages

An average, also called an **arithmetic mean**, is a number that *typifies* a group of numbers, a measure of central tendency. You come into contact with averages on a regular basis: your bowling average, the average grade on a test, the average number of hours you work per week.

To calculate an average, add up the number of items being averaged and divide by the number of items.

Example: What is the average of 6, 10, and 20?
Solution: Add the three numbers together and divide by 3: $\frac{6 + 10 + 20}{3} = 12$

Shortcut

Here's a neat shortcut for some average problems.

- Look at the numbers being averaged. If they are equally spaced, like 5, 10, 15, 20, and 25, then the average is the number in the middle, or 15 in this case.
- If there is an even number of such numbers, say 10, 20, 30, and 40, then there is no middle number. In this case, the average is half-way between the two middle numbers. In this case, the average is half-way between 20 and 30, or 25.
- If the numbers are almost evenly spaced, you can probably estimate the average without going to the trouble of actually computing it. For example, the average of 10, 20, and 32 is just a little more than 20, the middle number.

Try these average questions.

81. Bob's bowling scores for the last five games were 180, 182, 184, 186, and 188. What was his average bowling score?
   a. 182
   b. 183
   c. 184
   d. 185

82. Conroy averaged 30 miles an hour for the two hours he drove in town and 60 miles an hour for the two hours he drove on the highway. What was his average speed in miles per hour?

    a. 18

    b. $22\frac{1}{2}$

    c. 45

    d. 60

83. There are 10 females and 20 males in a history class. If the females achieved an average score of 85 and the males achieved an average score of 95, what was the class average? (Hint: Don't fall for the trap of taking the average of 85 and 95; there are more 95s being averaged than 85s, so the average is closer to 95.)

    a. $90\frac{2}{3}$

    b. $91\frac{2}{3}$

    c. 92

    d. $92\frac{2}{3}$

▶ Geometry

Typically, there are very few geometry problems on the math sections. The problems that are included tend to cover the basics: lines, angles, triangles, rectangles, squares, and circles. You may be asked to find the area or perimeter of a particular shape or the size of an angle. The arithmetic involved is pretty simple, so all you really need are a few definitions and formulas.

Practice Problems in Geometry

Try your hand at these sample problems.

Glossary of Geometry Terms

Angle	two rays with a common endpoint called a vertex. There are four types of angles:
	Acute: less than 90°
	Obtuse: more than 90°
	Right: 90°
	Straight: 180°
Circle	set of all points that are the same distance from the center.
	Area = πr^2
	Circumference = $2\pi r$
	($\pi = 3.14$; r = radius)
Circumference	distance around a circle. (See *circle*)

radius

Diameter   a line through the center of a circle. The diameter is twice the length of the radius. (See *circle, radius*)

Line   extends endlessly in both directions. It is referred to by a letter at the end of it or by two points on it. Thus, the line below may be referred to as line *l* or as $\overrightarrow{AB}$.

$$\begin{array}{cc} & A & B \\ l & \longleftrightarrow \end{array}$$

Parallel lines   two lines in the same plane that do not intersect.
       l || *m*

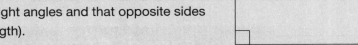

l _____

m _____

Perimeter   distance around a figure, such as a triangle or a rectangle. The perimeter of a circle is called its *circumference.*

       Perimeter = sum of length of all sides

Perpendicular lines   two lines in the same plane that intersect to form four right angles. (See *right angle*)

Point   has a location but no size or dimension. It is referred to by a letter close to it, like this: • *A*

Radius   line segment from the center to any point on a circle. The radius is half the diameter. (See *circle, diameter*)

Rectangle   four-sided figure with a right angle and both pairs of opposite sides parallel (which implies that all four sides are right angles and that opposite sides are equal in length).

       Area = *length × width*
       Perimeter = 2 × *length* + 2 × *width*

Square   rectangle with four equal sides (See *rectangle*).

       Area = (*side*)^2
       Perimeter = 4 × *side*

Triangle   three-sided figure.

       Area = $\frac{1}{2}$(*base × height*)
       Perimeter = sum of the lengths of all three sides
       Angles: The sum of the three angles of a triangle is always 180°.

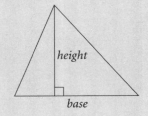

Practice Problems in Geometry

Try these sample problems.

84. What is the area in inches of a triangle with base 10″ and height 8″?
   a. 80
   b. 40
   c. 20
   d. 10

85. Find the perimeter of a triangle with sides of length 3, 4, and 5 units.
   a. 60 units
   b. 20 units
   c. 12 units
   d. 9 units

86. If the area of a square field measures 256 square feet, how many feet of fencing are needed to completely surround the field?
   a. 256
   b. 128
   c. 64
   d. It cannot be determined.

87. The length of a rectangle is twice its width. If the perimeter of the rectangle is 30 units, what is the width of the rectangle?
   a. 30
   b. 20
   c. 15
   d. 5

88. A circular opening has a diameter of $8\frac{1}{2}$ inches. What is the radius in inches of a circular disk that will exactly fit into the opening?
   a. 17
   b. 8.5
   c. 8
   d. 4.25

89. The radius of a hoop is 10″. If you roll the hoop along a straight path through 6 complete revolutions, approximately how far will it roll, in inches? (Use a value of 3.14 for π.)
   a. 31.4
   b. 62.8
   c. 188.4
   d. 376.8

▶ Algebra

Algebra questions do not appear on every test. However, when they do, they typically cover the material you learned in pre-algebra or in the first few months of your high school algebra course. Popular topics for algebra questions include:

- solving equations
- positive and negative numbers
- algebraic expressions

What Is Algebra?

Algebra is a way to express and solve problems using numbers and symbols. These symbols, called *unknowns* or *variables,* are letters of the alphabet that are used to represent numbers.

   For example, let's say you are asked to find out what number, when added to 3, gives you a total of 5. Using algebra, you could express the problem as $x + 3 = 5$. The variable x represents the number you are trying to find.

   Here's another example, but this one uses only variables. To find the distance traveled, multiply the rate of travel (speed) by the amount of time traveled: $d = r \times t$. The variable d stands for *distance,* r stands for *rate,* and t stands for *time.*

   In algebra, the variables may take on different values. In other words, they *vary,* and that's why they're called *variables.*

Operations

Algebra uses the same operations as arithmetic: addition, subtraction, multiplication, and division. In arithmetic, we might say $3 + 4 = 7$, while in algebra we would talk about two numbers whose values we don't know that add up to 7, or $x + y = 7$. Here's how each operation translates to algebra:

ALGEBRAIC OPERATIONS	
The sum of two numbers	$x + y$
The difference of two numbers	$x - y$
The product of two numbers	$x \times y$ or $x \bullet y$ or xy
The quotient of two numbers	$\frac{x}{y}$

Equations

An equation is a mathematical sentence stating that two quantities are equal. For example:

$$2x = 10$$
$$x + 5 = 8$$

The idea is to find a replacement for the unknown that will make the sentence true. That's called *solving* the equation. Thus, in the first example, $x = 5$ because $2 \times 5 = 10$. In the second example, $x = 3$ because $3 + 5 = 8$.

Sometimes you can solve an equation by inspection, as with the above examples. Other equations may be more complicated and require a step-by-step solution, for example:

$$\frac{n+2}{4+1} = 3$$

The general approach is to consider an equation like a balance scale, with both sides equally balanced. Essentially, whatever you do to one side, you must also do to the other side to maintain the balance. Thus, if you were to add 2 to the left side, you would also have to add 2 to the right side.

Let's apply this *balance* concept to our complicated equation above. Remembering that we want to solve it for *n,* we must somehow rearrange it so the *n* is isolated on one side of the equation. Its value will then be on the other side. Looking at the equation, you can see that *n* has been increased by 2 and then divided by 4 and ultimately added to 1. Therefore, we will undo these operations to isolate *n.*

Begin by subtracting 1 from both sides of the equation:

$$\frac{n+2}{4} + 1 = 3$$
$$\underline{ -1 \qquad -1}$$
$$\frac{n+2}{4} = 2$$

Next, multiply both sides by 4:

$$4 \times \frac{n+2}{4} = 2 \times 4$$
$$n + 2 = 8$$

Finally, subtract 2 from both sides:

$$\underline{-2 \qquad -2}$$

This isolates *n* and solves the equation:

$$n = 6$$

Notice that each operation in the original equation was undone by using the inverse operation. That is, addition was undone by subtraction, and division was undone by multiplication. In general, each operation can be undone by its *inverse:*

ALGEBRAIC INVERSES	
Operation	**Inverse**
Addition	Subtraction
Subtraction	Addition
Multiplication	Division
Division	Multiplication

After you solve an equation, check your work by plugging the answer back into the original equation to make sure it balances. Let's see what happens when we plug 6 in for *n:*

$$\frac{6+2}{4} + 1 = 3$$
$$\frac{8}{4} + 1 = 3$$
$$2 + 1 = 3$$
$$3 = 3$$

Solve each equation for *x:*

90. $x + 5 = 12$

91. $3x + 6 = 18$

92. $\frac{1}{4}x = 7$

Positive and Negative Numbers

Positive and negative numbers, also known as *signed* numbers, are best shown as points along the number line:

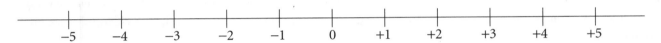

Numbers to the left of 0 are *negative* and those to the right are *positive.* Zero is neither negative nor positive. If a number is written without a sign, it is assumed to be *positive.* Notice that when you are on the negative side of the number line, numbers with bigger values are actually smaller. For example, −5 is *less than* −2. You come into contact with negative numbers more often than you might think; for example, very cold temperatures are recorded as negative numbers.

As you move to the right along the number line, the numbers get larger. Mathematically, to indicate that one number, say 4, is *greater than* another number, say −2, the *greater than* sign (>) is used:

$$4 > -2$$

On the other hand, to say that −2 is *less than* 4, we use the *less than* sign, (<):

$$-2 < 4$$

Arithmetic with Positive and Negative Numbers

The table below illustrates the rules for doing arithmetic with signed numbers. Notice that when a negative number follows an operation (as it does in the second example below), it is enclosed in parentheses to avoid confusion.

RULE	EXAMPLE
Addition	
If both numbers have the same sign, just add them. The answer has the same sign as the numbers being added. If both numbers have different signs, subtract the smaller number from the larger. The answer has the same sign as the larger number. If both numbers are the same but have opposite signs, the sum is zero.	$3 + 5 = 8$ $-3 + (-5) = -8$ $-3 + 5 = 2$ $3 + (-5) = -2$ $3 + (-3) = 0$
Subtraction	
Change the sign of the number to be subtracted and then add as above.	$3 - 5 = 3 + (-5) = -2$ $-3 - 5 = -3 + (-5) = -8$ $-3 - (-5) = -3 + 5 = 2$
Multiplication	
Multiply the numbers together. If both numbers have the same sign, the answer is positive; otherwise, it is negative.	$3 \times 5 = 15$ $-3 \times (-5) = 15$ $-3 \times 5 = -15$ $3 \times (-5) = -15$
If one number is zero, the answer is zero.	$3 \times 0 = 0$
Division	
Divide the numbers. If both numbers have the same sign, the answer is positive; otherwise, it is negative.	$15 \div 3 = 5$ $-15 \div (-3) = 5$ $15 \div (-3) = -5$ $-15 \div 3 = -5$
If the top number is zero, the answer is zero.	$0 \div 3 = 0$

When more than one arithmetic operation appears, you must know the correct sequence in which to perform the operations. For example, do you know what to do first to calculate $2 + 3 \times 4$? You're right if you said, "multiply first." The correct answer is 14. If you add first, you will get the wrong answer of 20. The correct sequence of operations is:

1. parentheses
2. exponents
3. multiplication
4. division
5. addition
6. subtraction

If you remember this saying, you will know the order of operations: **Please Excuse My Dear Aunt Sally.**

Even when signed numbers appear in an equation, the step-by-step solution works exactly as it does for positive numbers. You just have to remember the arithmetic rules for negative numbers. For example, let's solve $14x + 2 = 5$.

1. Subtract 2 from both sides:

$$-14x + 2 = -5$$
$$\underline{-2 \quad -2}$$
$$-14x = -7$$

2. Divide both sides by -14:

$$-14x \div -14 = -7 \div -14$$
$$x = \tfrac{1}{2}$$

Now try these problems with signed numbers. Solve for x.

93. $1 - 3 \times (-4) = x$

94. $-3x + 6 = -18$

95. $\frac{x}{-4} + 3 = -7$

Algebraic Expressions

An algebraic expression is a group of numbers, unknowns, and arithmetic operations, like: $3x - 2y$. This one may be translated as, "3 times some number minus 2 times another number." To *evaluate* an algebraic expression, replace each variable with its value. For example, if $x = 5$ and $y = 4$, we would evaluate $3x - 2y$ as follows:

$$3(5) - 2(4) = 15 - 8 = 7$$

Evaluate these expressions.

96. $4a + 3b$; $a = 2$ and $b = -1$

97. $3mn - 4m + 2n$; $m = 3$ and $n = -3$

98. $-2x - \frac{1}{2}y + 4z$; $x = 5$, $y = -4$, and $z = 6$

99. The volume of a cylinder is given by the formula $V = \pi r^2 h$, where r is the radius of the base and h is the height of the cylinder. What is the volume of a cylinder with a base radius of 3 and height of 4? (Leave π in your answer.)

100. If $x = 3$, what is the value of $3x - x$?

▶ Answers

Word Problems

1. a.
2. d.
3. d.
4. d.

Fractions

5. $\frac{1}{4}$
6. $\frac{2}{5}$
7. $\frac{3}{8}$
8. 10
9. 6
10. 200
11. $\frac{11}{12}$
12. $\frac{55}{24}$ or $2\frac{7}{24}$
13. $7\frac{1}{4}$
14. $\frac{2}{15}$
15. $\frac{1}{8}$
16. $\frac{19}{12}$ or $1\frac{7}{12}$
17. a.
18. b.
19. $\frac{2}{15}$
20. $\frac{8}{35}$
21. $\frac{2}{3}$
22. $\frac{26}{15}$ or $1\frac{11}{15}$
23. 15
24. $\frac{33}{2}$ or $16\frac{1}{2}$
25. c.
26. d.
27. c.
28. $\frac{1}{2}$
29. $5\frac{1}{2}$
30. $\frac{1}{5}$
31. $\frac{45}{28}$ or $1\frac{17}{28}$
32. b.
33. d.
34. b.

Decimals

35. $\frac{5}{1,000}$ or $\frac{1}{200}$
36. $3\frac{12}{25}$
37. $123\frac{456}{1,000}$ or $123\frac{57}{125}$
38. 4
39. 8.305
40. 0.907
41. 1.456
42. b.
43. d.
44. 0.03
45. 0.3392
46. 0.70104
47. d.
48. d.
49. 1.4
50. 128
51. 572
52. 1,400
53. b.
54. c.

Percents

55. 45%
56. 0.8%
57. 16.67% or $16\frac{2}{3}$%
58. 0.12
59. 0.875
60. 2.5
61. 12.5% or $12\frac{1}{2}$%
62. 52%
63. 58.33% or $58\frac{1}{3}$%
64. $\frac{19}{20}$
65. $\frac{3}{8}$

66. $\frac{5}{4}$ or $1\frac{1}{4}$
67. $\frac{1}{4}$ or .25
68. 9.1
69. $37\frac{1}{2}$ or 37.5
70. 75
71. 50%
72. $33\frac{1}{3}$%
73. 300%
74. 100
75. 8
76. 10
77. b.
78. c.
79. c.
80. d.

Averages

81. c.
82. c.
83. b.

Geometry

84. b.
85. c.
86. c.
87. d.
88. d.
89. d.

Algebra

90. 7
91. 4
92. 28
93. 13
94. 8
95. 40
96. 5
97. −45
98. 16
99. 36π
100. 6

Math Practice

CHAPTER SUMMARY

This chapter gives you opportunity for more practice with math.

f you feel like you could use some more practice with fractions, decimals, ratios, percentages, and word problems, try the problems in this chapter. The answers are given at the end. If there is a specific type of math
question that gives you trouble, go back to Chapter 6 and review the rules. Remember, the more math exercises you do, the closer you are to mastering the two math sections of the ASVAB that count toward the Armed
Forces Qualifying Test score—Arithmetic Reasoning and Mathematics Knowledge.

▶ Arithmetic Reasoning

1.	ⓐ	ⓑ	ⓒ	ⓓ	7.	ⓐ	ⓑ	ⓒ	ⓓ	13.	ⓐ	ⓑ	ⓒ	ⓓ
2.	ⓐ	ⓑ	ⓒ	ⓓ	8.	ⓐ	ⓑ	ⓒ	ⓓ	14.	ⓐ	ⓑ	ⓒ	ⓓ
3.	ⓐ	ⓑ	ⓒ	ⓓ	9.	ⓐ	ⓑ	ⓒ	ⓓ	15.	ⓐ	ⓑ	ⓒ	ⓓ
4.	ⓐ	ⓑ	ⓒ	ⓓ	10.	ⓐ	ⓑ	ⓒ	ⓓ	16.	ⓐ	ⓑ	ⓒ	ⓓ
5.	ⓐ	ⓑ	ⓒ	ⓓ	11.	ⓐ	ⓑ	ⓒ	ⓓ	17.	ⓐ	ⓑ	ⓒ	ⓓ
6.	ⓐ	ⓑ	ⓒ	ⓓ	12.	ⓐ	ⓑ	ⓒ	ⓓ					

▶ Mathematics Knowledge

18.	ⓐ	ⓑ	ⓒ	ⓓ	26.	ⓐ	ⓑ	ⓒ	ⓓ	34.	ⓐ	ⓑ	ⓒ	ⓓ
19.	ⓐ	ⓑ	ⓒ	ⓓ	27.	ⓐ	ⓑ	ⓒ	ⓓ	35.	ⓐ	ⓑ	ⓒ	ⓓ
20.	ⓐ	ⓑ	ⓒ	ⓓ	28.	ⓐ	ⓑ	ⓒ	ⓓ	36.	ⓐ	ⓑ	ⓒ	ⓓ
21.	ⓐ	ⓑ	ⓒ	ⓓ	29.	ⓐ	ⓑ	ⓒ	ⓓ	37.	ⓐ	ⓑ	ⓒ	ⓓ
22.	ⓐ	ⓑ	ⓒ	ⓓ	30.	ⓐ	ⓑ	ⓒ	ⓓ	38.	ⓐ	ⓑ	ⓒ	ⓓ
23.	ⓐ	ⓑ	ⓒ	ⓓ	31.	ⓐ	ⓑ	ⓒ	ⓓ	39.	ⓐ	ⓑ	ⓒ	ⓓ
24.	ⓐ	ⓑ	ⓒ	ⓓ	32.	ⓐ	ⓑ	ⓒ	ⓓ	40.	ⓐ	ⓑ	ⓒ	ⓓ
25.	ⓐ	ⓑ	ⓒ	ⓓ	33.	ⓐ	ⓑ	ⓒ	ⓓ					

▶ Arithmetic Reasoning

1. Derek earns $64.00 per day and spends $4.00 per day on transportation. What fraction of Derek's daily earnings does he spend on transportation?

   a. $\frac{1}{32}$

   b. $\frac{1}{18}$

   c. $\frac{1}{16}$

   d. $\frac{1}{8}$

2. A bread recipe calls for $6\frac{1}{2}$ cups of flour, but Leonard has only $5\frac{1}{3}$ cups. How much more flour does Leonard need?

   a. $\frac{2}{3}$ cup

   b. $\frac{5}{6}$ cup

   c. $1\frac{1}{6}$ cups

   d. $1\frac{1}{4}$ cups

3. Over a period of four days, Roberto drove a total of 956.58 miles. What is the average number of miles Roberto drove each day?

   a. 239.145

   b. 239.2

   c. 249.045

   d. 249.45

4. Eighteen percent of Centerville's total yearly $1,250,000 budget is spent on road repairs. How much money does Centerville spend on road repairs each year?

   a. $11,250

   b. $22,500

   c. $112,500

   d. $225,000

5. In January, Bart's electricity bill was $35.00. In February, his bill was $42.00. By what percent did his electricity bill increase?

   a. 7%

   b. 12%

   c. 16%

   d. 20%

6. On a state road map, one inch represents 20 miles. Denise wants to travel from Garden City to Marshalltown, which is a distance of $4\frac{1}{4}$ inches on the map. How many miles will Denise travel?

   a. 45

   b. 82

   c. 85

   d. 90

7. In the freshman class, the ratio of in-state students to out-of-state students is 15 to 2. If there are 750 in-state students in the class, how many out-of-state students are there?

   a. 100

   b. 112

   c. 130

   d. 260

8. The high temperatures for the first five days in September are as follows: Sunday, 72°; Monday, 79°; Tuesday, 81°; Wednesday 74°; Thursday, 68°. What is the average (mean) high temperature for those five days?

   a. 73.5°

   b. 74°

   c. 74.8°

   d. 75.1°

9. A bag contains 105 jelly beans: 23 white, 23 red, 14 purple, 26 yellow, and 19 green ones. What is the probability of selecting either a yellow or a green jelly bean?

   a. $\frac{3}{7}$

   b. $\frac{1}{6}$

   c. $\frac{1}{12}$

   d. $\frac{2}{9}$

10. A can contains 200 mixed nuts: almonds, cashews, and peanuts. If the probability of choosing an almond is $\frac{1}{10}$ and the probability of choosing a cashew is $\frac{1}{4}$, how many peanuts are in the can?

   a. 90

   b. 110

   c. 130

   d. 186

11. Tarik spent $46.53 on groceries. If he handed the checkout clerk three $20 bills, how much change should he receive?

   a. $13.47

   b. $14.47

   c. $14.57

   d. $16.53

12. Colleen purchased a large bag of apples. She used $\frac{1}{2}$ of them to make applesauce. Of those she had left, she used $\frac{3}{4}$ to make an apple pie. When she was finished, she had only three apples left. How many apples were there to begin with?

   a. 21

   b. 24

   c. 28

   d. 36

13. Of the 80 employees working on the road-construction crew, 35% worked overtime this week. How many employees did NOT work overtime?

   a. 28

   b. 45

   c. 52

   d. 56

14. If Lydia's height is $\frac{2}{a}$ of Francine's height and Francine is b inches tall, how tall is Lydia?

   a. $\frac{2}{ab}$

   b. $2(ab)$

   c. $2\frac{a}{b}$

   d. $\frac{2b}{a}$

15. A triangle has an area of 9 square inches. If its base is 3 inches, what is its height in inches?

   a. 3

   b. 4

   c. 6

   d. 12

16. What are the dimensions of a rectangular room with a perimeter of 42 feet if the long side is twice as long as the short side?

   a. 7 feet by 14 feet

   b. 8 feet by 16 feet

   c. 12 feet by 24 feet

   d. 14 feet by 28 feet

17. If the area of a square is 25 square feet, how long is one of its sides?

   a. 2.5 feet

   b. 5 feet

   c. 10 feet

   d. 12.5 feet

► Mathematics Knowledge

18. Name the fraction that indicates the shaded part of the figure below.

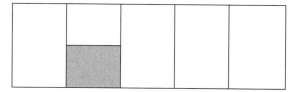

   a. $\frac{2}{5}$

   b. $\frac{1}{5}$

   c. $\frac{1}{8}$

   d. $\frac{1}{10}$

19. Four ounces is what fraction of a pound? (one pound = 16 ounces)

   a. $\frac{1}{3}$

   b. $\frac{3}{8}$

   c. $\frac{1}{4}$

   d. $\frac{1}{6}$

20. Which fraction is smallest?

   a. $\frac{3}{8}$

   b. $\frac{1}{4}$

   c. $\frac{5}{24}$

   d. $\frac{1}{6}$

21. What is the decimal value of $\frac{5}{8}$?

   a. 0.56

   b. 0.625

   c. 0.8

   d. 0.835

22. Raise $\frac{5}{9}$ to 36ths.

   a. $\frac{18}{36}$

   b. $\frac{20}{36}$

   c. $\frac{24}{36}$

   d. $\frac{30}{36}$

23. $1\frac{3}{4} + 3\frac{1}{2} =$

   a. $4\frac{1}{4}$

   b. $4\frac{3}{4}$

   c. $5\frac{1}{4}$

   d. $5\frac{1}{2}$

24. $4 - 1\frac{4}{5}$

   a. $2\frac{1}{5}$

   b. $2\frac{4}{5}$

   c. $3\frac{3}{10}$

   d. $3\frac{1}{5}$

25. $\frac{5}{8} \times \frac{4}{15} =$

   a. $\frac{1}{6}$

   b. $\frac{2}{5}$

   c. $\frac{9}{15}$

   d. $\frac{7}{45}$

26. $\frac{1}{2} \times 16 \times \frac{3}{8} =$

   a. $\frac{1}{4}$

   b. $2\frac{5}{16}$

   c. 3

   d. $4\frac{1}{4}$

27. If a $14\frac{3}{4}$ length of ribbon is cut into four equal pieces, how long will each piece be?

   a. $3\frac{1}{8}$

   b. $3\frac{1}{4}$

   c. $3\frac{5}{8}$

   d. $3\frac{11}{16}$

28. What is 0.7849 rounded to the nearest hundredth?

   a. 0.8

   b. 0.78

   c. 0.785

   d. 0.79

29. $2.36 + 14 + 0.083 =$

   a. 14.059

   b. 16.443

   c. 16.69

   d. 17.19

30. $1.5 - 0.188 =$

   a. 0.62

   b. 1.262

   c. 1.27

   d. 1.312

31. $12 - 0.92 + 4.6 =$

   a. 17.52

   b. 16.68

   c. 15.68

   d. 8.4

32. $2.39 \times 10,000 =$

   a. 239

   b. 2,390

   c. 23,900

   d. 239,000

33. $5 \times 0.0063 =$

   a. 0.0315

   b. 0.315

   c. 3.15

   d. 31.5

34. 45% is equal to what fraction?

   a. $\frac{4}{5}$

   b. $\frac{5}{8}$

   c. $\frac{25}{50}$

   d. $\frac{9}{20}$

35. 0.925 is equal to what percent?

   a. 925%

   b. 92.5%

   c. 9.25%

   d. 0.0925%

36. What is 12% of 60?

   a. 5

   b. 7.2

   c. 50

   d. 72

37. Of the 500 coins in a jar, 45 are quarters. What percent of the coins in the jar is quarters?

   a. 9%

   b. 9.5%

   c. 11.1%

   d. 15%

38. 16 is 20% of what number?

   a. 8

   b. 12.5

   c. 32

   d. 80

39. Which of the following is an obtuse angle?

a.

b.

c.

d.

40. What is the perimeter of the polygon below?

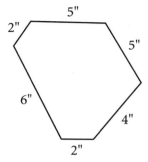

a. 24″
b. 25″
c. 27″
d. 32″

► Answers

Arithmetic Reasoning

1. c.
2. c.
3. a.
4. d.
5. d.
6. c.
7. a.
8. c.
9. a.
10. c.
11. a.
12. b.
13. c.
14. d.
15. c.
16. a.
17. b.

Mathematics Knowledge

18. d.
19. c.
20. d.
21. b.
22. b.
23. c.
24. a.
25. a.
26. c.
27. d.
28. b.
29. b.
30. d.
31. c.
32. c.
33. a.
34. d.
35. b.
36. b.
37. a.
38. d.
39. b.
40. a.

Word Knowledge Review

CHAPTER SUMMARY

This chapter will help you improve your vocabulary skills so that you can score higher on the Word Knowledge section of the ASVAB.

The Word Knowledge subtest of the ASVAB is basically a vocabulary test. Combined with the Paragraph Comprehension score, Word Knowledge helps make up your Verbal Equivalent score—it is one of the four subtests that determines whether you will be allowed to enlist. Your ability to understand your training materials depends in part on your reading comprehension and vocabulary skills.

There are two different kinds of questions on the Word Knowledge subtest:

- **Synonyms**—identifying words that mean the same as the given words
- **Context**—determining the meaning of a word or phrase by noting how it is used in a sentence or paragraph

▶ Synonym Questions

A word is a **synonym** of another word if it has the same or nearly the same meaning as the other word. Test questions often ask you to find the synonym or antonym of a word. If you're lucky, the word will be surrounded by a sentence that helps you guess what the word means. If you're less lucky, you will just get the word, and then you have to figure out what the word means without any context.

Questions that ask for synonyms can be tricky because they require you to recognize the meaning of several words that may be unfamiliar—not only the words in the questions but also the answer choices. Usually the best strategy is to *look* at the structure of the word and to *listen* for its sound. See if a part of a word looks familiar. Think of other words you know that have similar key elements. How could those words be related?

Synonym Practice Questions

Try identifying the word parts and related words in these sample synonym questions. Circle the word that means the same or about the same as the italicized word. Answers and explanations appear right after the questions.

1. *incoherent* answer
   a. not understandable
   b. not likely
   c. undeniable
   d. challenging

2. *ambiguous* questions
   a. meaningless
   b. difficult
   c. simple
   d. vague

3. covered with *debris*
   a. good excuses
   b. transparent material
   c. scattered rubble
   d. protective material

4. *inadvertently* left
   a. mistakenly
   b. purposely
   c. cautiously
   d. carefully

5. *exorbitant* prices
   a. expensive
   b. unexpected
   c. reasonable
   d. outrageous

6. *compatible* workers
   a. gifted
   b. competitive
   c. harmonious
   d. experienced

7. *belligerent* attitude
   a. hostile
   b. reasonable
   c. instinctive
   d. friendly

Answers to Synonym Practice Questions

The explanations are important because they show you how to go about choosing a synonym if you don't know the word.

1. **a.** *Incoherent* means *not understandable*. To *cohere* means to *connect*. A coherent answer connects or makes sense. The prefix *in-* means *not*.

2. **d.** *Ambiguous* questions are *vague* or uncertain. The key part of this word is *ambi-*, which means *two* or *both*. An ambiguous question can be taken two ways.

3. **c.** *Debris* are scattered fragments and trash.

4. **a.** *Inadvertently* means *by mistake*. The key element in this word is the prefix *in-*, which usually means *not*, or *the opposite of*.

5. **d.** The key element here is *ex-*, which means *out of* or *away from*. Exorbitant literally means "out of orbit." An *exorbitant* price would be an *outrageous* one.

6. c. *Compatible* means *harmonious.*

7. a. The key element in this word is the root *belli-,* which means *warlike.* The synonym choice, then, is *hostile.*

Context Questions

Context is the surrounding text in which a word is used. Most people use context to help them determine the meaning of an unknown word. A vocabulary question that gives you a sentence around the vocabulary word is usually easier to answer than one with little or no context. The surrounding text can help you as you look for synonyms for the specified words in the sentences.

The best way to take meaning from context is to look for key words in sentences or paragraphs that convey the meaning of the text. If nothing else, the context will give you a means to eliminate wrong answer choices that clearly don't fit. The process of elimination will often leave you with the correct answer.

Context Practice Questions

Try these sample questions. Circle the word that best describes the meaning of the italicized word in the sentence.

8. The maintenance workers were *appalled* by the filthy, cluttered condition of the building.
  a. horrified
  b. amused
  c. surprised
  d. dismayed

9. Even though she seemed rich, the defendant claimed to be *destitute.*
  a. wealthy
  b. ambitious
  c. solvent
  d. poor

10. Though she was *distraught* over losing her keys, the woman was calm enough to remember she had a spare set.
  a. punished
  b. distracted
  c. composed
  d. anguished

11. The evil criminal expressed no *remorse* for his actions.
  a. sympathy
  b. regret
  c. reward
  d. complacency

Answers to Context Practice Questions

Check to see whether you were able to pick out the key words that help you define the target word, as well as whether you got the right answer.

8. a. The key words *filthy* and *cluttered* signify horror rather than the milder emotions described by the other choices.

9. d. The key word here is *rich,* but this is a clue by contrast. The introductory *even though* signals that you should look for the opposite of the idea of having financial resources.

10. d. The key words here are *though* and *losing her keys,* signaling that you are looking for an opposite of *calm* in describing the woman. The only word strong enough to match the situation is *anguish.*

11. b. *Remorse* means *regret* for one's actions. The part of the word here to beware of is the prefix *re-.* It doesn't signify anything in this word, though it often means again or back. Don't be confused by the two choices that also contain the prefix *re-.* The strategy here is to see which word sounds better in the sentence. The key words are *evil* and *no,* indicating that you are looking for something that shows no repentance.

Be very careful not to be confused by the sound of words that may mislead you. Be sure to look at the word carefully, and pay attention to the structure and appearance of the word as well as its sound. You may be used to hearing English words spoken with an accent. The sounds of those words may be misleading in choosing a correct answer.

Word Parts

The best way to improve your vocabulary is to learn word parts: roots, which are the main part of the word; prefixes, which go before the root word; or suffixes, which go after. Any of these elements can carry meaning or change the use of a word in a sentence. For instance, the suffix -s or -es can change the meaning of a noun from singular to plural: *boy, boys.* The prefix *un-* can change the meaning of a root word to its opposite: *necessary, unnecessary.*

In the sections on **prefixes** and **suffixes** are some of the word elements seen most often in vocabulary tests. Simply reading them and their examples for five to ten minutes a day will give you the quick recognition you need to make a good association with the meaning of an unfamiliar word.

Prefixes

In order to be able to unlock the meaning of many words in our language, it is useful for you to understand what a prefix is. A prefix is a word part at the beginning of a word that changes or adds to the meaning of the root word in some way. By learning some common prefixes, you will learn to recognize many unfamiliar words. After you have completed the exercises in this chapter, you will become acquainted with the meanings suggested by some of the more common prefixes, which will improve your reading, speaking, and listening vocabularies.

antecedent   (an·ti·ˈsēd·ənt)
prefix: **ante** means before
(*adj.*)
going before in time
The event was _____ to the Civil War.

antipathy   (an·ˈtip·ə·thē)
prefix: **anti** means against
(*noun*)
revulsion; any object of strong dislike
The child had an _____ toward snakes.

circumvent   (sər·kəm·ˈvent)
prefix: **circum** and **circ** mean around
(*verb*)
to go around; to catch in a trap; to gain superiority over; to prevent from happening
Police tried to _____ the riot by moving the crowd along.

consensus   (kən·ˈsen·səs)
prefix: **con** means with, together
(*noun*)
agreement, especially in opinion
The committee reached _____ about gun control.

controversy   (ˈkon·trə·ver·sē)
prefix: **contr** means against
(*noun*)
a discussion of a question in which opposing views clash
There is a _____ about building nuclear power plants.

decimate　　('des·i·mat)
prefix: **dec** means ten
(*verb*)
to destroy or kill a large portion of something; to take
　　or destroy a tenth part of something
Caterpillars can ＿＿＿＿＿ trees.

demote　　(di·mōt)
prefix: **de** means down, away from
(*verb*)
to lower in grade or position
Upper ranked officers can ＿＿＿＿＿ a lower ranked
　　person.

disinterested　　(dis·'in·tər·est·ed)
prefix: **dis** means not, opposite of
(*adj.*)
not motivated by personal interest or selfish motives
A loyal citizen is ＿＿＿＿＿.

euphemism　　('u·fə·mizm)
prefix: **eu** means good, well
(*noun*)
the use of a word or phrase that is considered less dis-
　　tasteful or offensive than another
"She is at rest" is a ＿＿＿＿＿ for "she is dead."

exorbitant　　(ek·'zor·bi·tənt)
prefix: **ex** means out of, away from
(*adj.*)
going beyond what is reasonable and proper
The colonists rebelled against ＿＿＿＿＿ taxes.

illegible　　(i·'lej·ə·bəl)
prefix: **il** means not, opposite
(*adj.*)
not able to be read
The student had to rewrite the ＿＿＿＿＿ paper.

intermittent　　(in·tər·'mit·ənt)
prefix: **inter** means between
(*adj.*)
stopping and starting again at intervals
The weather forecaster predicted ＿＿＿＿＿ showers.

malevolent　　(mə·'lev·ə·lent)
prefix: **mal** means bad
(*adj.*)
having an evil disposition toward others
A ＿＿＿＿＿ person rejoices in the misfortune of
　　others.

precursor　　(prē·'kər·sər)
prefix: **pre** means before
(*noun*)
a forerunner, a harbinger; one who or that which
　　goes before
Calmness is usually a ＿＿＿＿＿ to a storm.

prognosis　　(prog·'nō·sis)
prefix: **pro** means before
(*noun*)
a forecast; especially in medicine
The injured animal's ＿＿＿＿＿ for recovery is good.

retrospect　　('ret·rō·spekt)
prefix: **retro** means back, again
(*verb*)
to think about the past
(*noun*)
looking back on or thinking about things past
In ＿＿＿＿＿, the world leader wished he had acted
　　differently.

subordinate (sub·'or·din·it)
prefix: **sub** means under
(*adj.*)
inferior to or placed below another in rank, power, or importance
(*noun*) (sub·'or·din·it)
a person or thing of lesser power or importance than another
(*verb*) (sub·'or·din·āt)
to treat as inferior or less important
The wise president treated her _____ with respect.

synthesis ('sin·thə·sis)
prefix: **syn** or **sym** means with or together
(*noun*)
putting of two or more things to together to form a whole
In chemistry, the process of making a compound by joining elements together is called _____.

transcend (tran·'send)
prefix: **trans** means across
(*verb*)
to go beyond the limits of; to overstep; to exceed
A seeing eye dog enables blind people to _____ their disability.

trivial ('triv·ē·əl)
prefix: **tri** means three
(*adj.*)
of little worth or importance
The research scientist did not have time for _____ pursuits because he was so busy conducting important experiments.

Words in Context

The following exercise will help you figure out the meaning of some words from the previous list. Circle any context clues that help you figure out the meaning of the bold words.

In our country, the use of nuclear power as a viable source of energy has been an ongoing **controversy.** During the gas and oil shortages of the 1970s, energy prices were **exorbitant.** The federal government supported nuclear power as a new energy source that would be cost effective. Now, the president's National Energy Policy Report lists nuclear power as a safe and affordable alternative. Today, as in the past, many people have voiced their **antipathy** toward nuclear power plants, especially in the wake of the 1979 partial meltdown of the Three Mile Island nuclear power plant. At that time, scientists scrambled to **circumvent** a total meltdown in a facility that was designed to be fail-safe. There was great fear that the meltdown would be complete and **decimate** the area. Now, the federal government is once again promoting this alternative energy source.

Suffixes

Word endings that are added to the main part or root of words are called **suffixes.** Suffixes are word parts that signal how a word is being used in a sentence. You will note that each word in the list is a particular part of speech (*noun, verb, adjective,* or *adverb*). Suffixes often change the part of speech of a word.

For example, take the word *deferment* from the list below. A *deferment* is a noun that means a postponement. If the suffix (word ending *-ment*) is removed, the word becomes *defer,* and it is used as a verb meaning *to postpone.*

As a *verb* it appears as *defer*:
I will *defer* the payment until next month.

As a *noun* it appears as it is:
The bank gave him a *deferment.*

As an *adjective* it appears as *deferred*:
The *deferred* payment is due in one month.

The following table shows a list of common suffixes. They are divided into the parts of speech, or the "jobs" they suggest for words. In the last column, add at least one other word that uses the suffix, besides the examples in the word list.

NOUN ENDINGS			
Suffix	**Meaning**	**Examples**	**Your Word**
-tion	act or state of	retraction, contraction	
-ment	quality	deportment, impediment	
-ist	one who	anarchist, feminist	
-ism	state or doctrine of	barbarism, materialism	
-ity	state of being	futility, civility	
-ology	study of	biology	
-esence	state of	adolescence	
-y, -ry	state of	mimicry, trickery	

ADJECTIVE ENDINGS			
Suffix	**Meaning**	**Examples**	**Your Word**
-able	capable	perishable, flammable	
-ic	causing, making	nostalgic, fatalistic	
-ian	one who is or does	tactician, patrician	
-ile	pertaining to	senile, servile	
-ious	having the quality of	religious, glorious	
-ive	having the nature of	sensitive, divisive	
-less	without	guileless, reckless	

VERB ENDINGS			
Suffix	**Meaning**	**Examples**	**Your Word**
-ize	to bring about	colonize, plagiarize	
-ate	to make	decimate, tolerate	
-ify	to make	beautify, electrify	

agrarian　(ə·′grer·ē·ən)
suffix: **-ian** means one who is or does
(*adj.*)
having to do with agriculture or farming
The farmer loved his _____ life.

antagonist　(an·′ta·gə·nist)
suffix: **-ist** means one who
(*noun*)
one that contends with or opposes another
In the movie *Batman*, the Joker is Batman's _____.

bigotry　(′big·ə·trē)
suffix: **-ry** means state of
(*noun*)
unreasonable zeal in favor of a party, sect, or opinion; excessive prejudice
_____ can lead to malevolent actions.

consummate   ('kon·səm·māt)
suffix: **-ate** means to make
(*verb*)
to complete; to carry to the utmost degree
The business woman needed to _____ the deal
    quickly.

copious   ('cōp·ē·əs)
suffix: **-ious** means having the quality of
(*adj.*)
abundant; plentiful; in great quantities
A _____ amount of sunshine is predicted for the
    summer.

cryptic   ('krip·tik)
suffix: **-ic** means causing
(*adj.*)
hidden; secret; having a hidden or ambiguous
    meaning
The detective uncovered the meaning of the
    _____ message.

deferment   (di·'fər·mənt)
suffix: **-ment** means quality of
(*noun*)
the act of putting off or delaying; postponement
The bank offered the struggling college graduate a
    _____ on his student loan payment.

furtive   ('fər·tiv)
suffix: **-ive** means having the nature of
(*adj.*)
done in a stealthy manner; sly and underhanded
The two criminals who were in cahoots gave each
    other _____ looks behind the detective's
    back.

laudable   ('law·də·bəl)
suffix: **-able** means capable of
(*adj.*)
praiseworthy
Her dedication and ability to rehabilitate the injured
    is _____.

geology   (jē·'ä·lə·jē)
suffix: **-ology** means study of
(*noun*)
the study of the history of the Earth and its life,
    especially as recorded in rocks
The _____ major traveled to Mt. Etna to exam-
    ine the effects of the volcano's most recent
    eruption.

minimize   ('mi·nə·mīz)
suffix: **-ize** means to subject to an action
(*verb*)
to play down; to keep to a minimum
The man tried to _____ his involvement in the
    trial so that he would not be implicated in the
    scandal.

mutation   (mū·'tā·shən)
suffix: **-tion** means action of, state of
(*noun*)
the act or process of changing
Scientists research gene _____ in fruit flies to
    see how genes change from one generation to
    the next.

obsolescence   (äb·sə·'les·ens)
suffix: **-escence** means state of
(*noun*)
the state of being outdated
With the advent of the personal computer, the type-
    writer has been in _____ for many years.

parity   ('par·i·tē)
suffix: **-ity** means state of being
(*noun*)
the state or condition of being the same in power,
    value, or rank; equality
Women and minorities continue to fight for
    _____ in the workplace.

pragmatism ('prag·mə·tizm)
suffix: **-ism** means state or doctrine of
(*noun*)
faith in the practical approach
The man's _____ enabled him to run a successful business.

provocative (prō·'vok·ə·tiv)
suffix: **-ive** means having the nature of
(*adj.*)
something that stirs up an action
The _____ words of the environmental activist
inspired many to go volunteer for the community clean-up day.

puerile ('pyoor·əl)
suffix: **-ile** means pertaining to
(*adj.*)
childish, silly, immature
The teen's _____ actions at the party couldn't be
ignored.

rectify ('rek·ti·fī)
suffix: **-ify** means to make
(*verb*)
to make right; to correct
The newspaper tried to _____ the mistake by
correcting the misprint.

relentless (re·'lənt·les)
suffix: **-less** means without
(*adj.*)
harsh; unmoved by pity; unstoppable
She was _____ in her search for knowledge; she
read everything she could get her hands on.

venerate ('ven·ə·rāt)
suffix: **-ate** means to make
(*verb*)
to look upon with deep respect and reverence
Some cultures _____ their elders.

Words in Context

The following exercise will help you figure out the
meaning of some words from the previous list by looking at context clues. Circle any context clues that help
you figure out the meaning of the bold word.

The latest remake of *Planet of the Apes* develops the
theme of **bigotry** in a world where apes are the
dominant culture and humans are enslaved. **Parity**
between the two species is unthinkable because the
simians regard humans as inferior creatures. Leo,
the central character, is the story's protagonist. He
is a human astronaut who lands on a strange
planet where apes **venerate** their own kind by
offering praise and promotions for negative
actions taken against humans. Leo's **antagonist**,
General Thade, is the leader of the apes in this
bizarre culture, and encourages the mistreatment
of humans by apes. In General Thade's opinion,
extermination of the humans is a **laudable** cause
and he mounts a full-scale campaign to extermi-
nate humans from the planet.

More Vocabulary Practice Questions

Here is another set of practice exercises with samples of
each kind of question covered in this chapter. Answers
are at the end of the exercise.

Select the word that means the same or nearly the
same as the italicized word.

12. *congenial* company
   a. friendly
   b. dull
   c. tiresome
   d. angry

13. *conspicuous* mess
   a. secret
   b. notable
   c. visible
   d. boorish

- The key to answering vocabulary questions is to **notice and connect** what you do know to what you may not recognize.
- **Know your word parts.** You can recognize or make a good guess at the meanings of words when you see some suggested meaning in a root word, prefix, or suffix.
- **Use a process of elimination.** Think of how the word makes sense in the sentence.
- **Don't be confused by words that sound like other words**, but may have no relation to the word you need.

---

14. *meticulous* record-keeping
   a. dishonest
   b. casual
   c. painstaking
   d. careless

15. *superficial* wounds
   a. life-threatening
   b. bloody
   c. severe
   d. surface

16. *impulsive* actions
   a. cautious
   b. sudden
   c. courageous
   d. cowardly

17. *tactful* comments
   a. polite
   b. rude
   c. angry
   d. confused

Using the context, choose the word that means the same or nearly the same as the italicized word.

18. Though flexible about homework, the teacher was *adamant* that papers be in on time.
   a. liberal
   b. casual
   c. strict
   d. pliable

19. The condition of the room after the party was *deplorable.*
   a. regrettable
   b. pristine
   c. festive
   d. tidy

20. Though normally very *gregarious*, Martin was uncharacteristically shy and reserved when he attended the party.
   a. generous
   b. sociable
   c. stingy
   d. happy

**Answers to
Vocabulary Practice Questions**
   12. a.
   13. c.
   14. c.
   15. d.
   16. b.
   17. a.
   18. c.
   19. a.
   20. b.

Word Knowledge Practice

CHAPTER SUMMARY

This chapter gives you the opportunity for more practice with Word Knowledge questions.

I f you feel like you could use extra practice with synonym or context questions, complete the exercises in this chapter. The answers are given at the end. When you miss a question, look up that word in the dictionary, study the different parts of the word, and commit it to memory. It's a good idea to complete this chapter even if you feel you have strong vocabulary skills. You may learn a word or two—and that will help you pick up precious points on the Word Knowledge subtest of the ASVAB, which will count toward your Armed Forces Qualifying Test score.

▶ Word Knowledge Practice

1.	ⓐ	ⓑ	ⓒ	ⓓ	
2.	ⓐ	ⓑ	ⓒ	ⓓ	
3.	ⓐ	ⓑ	ⓒ	ⓓ	
4.	ⓐ	ⓑ	ⓒ	ⓓ	
5.	ⓐ	ⓑ	ⓒ	ⓓ	
6.	ⓐ	ⓑ	ⓒ	ⓓ	
7.	ⓐ	ⓑ	ⓒ	ⓓ	
8.	ⓐ	ⓑ	ⓒ	ⓓ	
9.	ⓐ	ⓑ	ⓒ	ⓓ	

10.	ⓐ	ⓑ	ⓒ	ⓓ
11.	ⓐ	ⓑ	ⓒ	ⓓ
12.	ⓐ	ⓑ	ⓒ	ⓓ
13.	ⓐ	ⓑ	ⓒ	ⓓ
14.	ⓐ	ⓑ	ⓒ	ⓓ
15.	ⓐ	ⓑ	ⓒ	ⓓ
16.	ⓐ	ⓑ	ⓒ	ⓓ
17.	ⓐ	ⓑ	ⓒ	ⓓ
18.	ⓐ	ⓑ	ⓒ	ⓓ

19.	ⓐ	ⓑ	ⓒ	ⓓ
20.	ⓐ	ⓑ	ⓒ	ⓓ
21.	ⓐ	ⓑ	ⓒ	ⓓ
22.	ⓐ	ⓑ	ⓒ	ⓓ
23.	ⓐ	ⓑ	ⓒ	ⓓ
24.	ⓐ	ⓑ	ⓒ	ⓓ
25.	ⓐ	ⓑ	ⓒ	ⓓ

▶ Word Knowledge

Choose the word or phrase that is closest in meaning to the underlined word.

1. Jerry liked to <u>antagonize</u> his sister by repeating everything she said.
   a. impress
   b. sympathize with
   c. irritate
   d. condescend to

2. She didn't want to be recognized, so Anna went <u>incognito</u> to the dance.
   a. in disguise
   b. without a date
   c. formally dressed
   d. casually dressed

3. I wanted the meal to be delicious, so I <u>perused</u> the recipe several times before I started cooking.
   a. wrote
   b. read
   c. prepared
   d. made

4. The sister tried to <u>circumvent</u> the issue by pointing out her brother's many failings.
   a. get above
   b. intensify
   c. bring into the open
   d. go around

5. <u>Caveat</u> most nearly means
   a. peace offering.
   b. appetizer.
   c. warning.
   d. excuse.

6. <u>Parity</u> most nearly means
   a. equality.
   b. mimicry.
   c. style of belief.
   d. current trend.

7. <u>Pundit</u> most nearly means
   a. private joke.
   b. expert.
   c. diplomat.
   d. folk dance.

8. <u>Narcissistic</u> most nearly means
   a. having an addictive personality.
   b. having a narcotic effect.
   c. self-absorbed.
   d. witty.

9. <u>Mesmerize</u> most nearly means
   a. to reign over others.
   b. to record in prose.
   c. to memorialize.
   d. to fascinate.

10. <u>Prospectus</u> most nearly means
   a. published business plan.
   b. the outlook from a mountain top.
   c. opening speech.
   d. professional playing field.

11. <u>Fiscal</u> most nearly means
   a. official.
   b. stated.
   c. financial.
   d. faithful.

12. The candidate for the position knew the <u>jargon</u> and had a pleasant demeanor.
   a. scientific specialty
   b. public policy issues
   c. language particular to the field
   d. behavior code

13. Surprisingly, the child had a <u>stoic</u> attitude toward the hours of homework assigned to her.
   a. tainted
   b. uncomplaining
   c. angry
   d. self-defeating

14. <u>Belligerent</u> most nearly means
   a. warlike.
   b. flighty.
   c. easily tired.
   d. beautiful.

15. <u>Retrospect</u> most nearly means
   a. analytic.
   b. careful.
   c. hindsight.
   d. a magnifying instrument.

16. <u>Subsidy</u> most nearly means
   a. the punishment of a criminal offense.
   b. the aftermath of a storm.
   c. money given in support of a cause or industry.
   d. a vote directly by the people.

17. <u>Cryptic</u> most nearly means
   a. mysterious.
   b. evil.
   c. a spy code.
   d. a tomb.

18. There was an <u>audible</u> sigh of relief when the rescuers brought the drowning man to the surface.
   a. incredible
   b. able to be heard
   c. worthy of praise
   d. able to be seen

19. Before setting out on the long hike, we made a <u>requisite</u> check for food and water supplies.
   a. required
   b. safe
   c. ample
   d. up-to-date

20. Her <u>vivacious</u> manner contrasted with the seriousness of her appearance.
   a. grave
   b. hostile
   c. joyous
   d. lively

21. He wanted to reread the recipe to <u>verify</u> the ingredients before starting to cook.
   a. confirm
   b. total
   c. analyze
   d. measure

22. The <u>loquacious</u> dinner guest dominated the conversation.
   a. intoxicated
   b. talkative
   c. silent
   d. greedy

23. The soap opera emphasized the <u>pathos</u>, rather than the humor, of family life.
 a. sentimental feeling
 b. turmoil
 c. activity
 d. horror

24. The <u>fluctuating</u> price of gas kept motorists guessing.
 a. changing
 b. inexpensive
 c. costly
 d. confusing

25. His <u>chronic</u> lateness was treated with humor by those who had known him for a long time.
 a. occasional
 b. constant
 c. unusual
 d. rare

▶ **Answers**

1. c.
2. a.
3. b.
4. d.
5. c.
6. a.
7. b.
8. c.
9. d.
10. a.
11. c.
12. c.
13. b.
14. a.
15. c.
16. c.
17. a.
18. b.
19. a.
20. d.
21. a.
22. b.
23. a.
24. a.
25. b.

10▶ Paragraph Comprehension Review

CHAPTER SUMMARY
Because reading is such a vital skill, the Armed Services Vocational Aptitude Battery includes a reading comprehension section that tests your ability to understand what you read. The tips and exercises in this chapter will help you improve your comprehension of written passages as well as of tables, charts, and graphs, so that you can increase your score in this area.

Memos, policies, procedures, reports—these are all things you will be expected to understand if you enlist in the armed services. Understanding written materials is part of almost any job. That's why the ASVAB attempts to measure this skill in applicants.

The Paragraph Comprehension subtest of the ASVAB is in multiple-choice format and asks questions based on brief passages, much like the standardized tests that are offered in schools. For that matter, almost all standardized test questions test your reading skills. After all, you can't answer the question if you can't read it. Similarly, you can't study your training materials or learn new procedures once you are on the job if you can't read well. So, reading comprehension is vital not only on the test but also for the rest of your career.

▶ Types of Reading Comprehension Questions

You have probably encountered reading comprehension questions before, where you are given a passage to read and then have to answer multiple-choice questions about it. This kind of question has advantages for you as a test taker: You don't have to know anything about the topic of the passage because you are being tested only on the information the passage provides.

But the disadvantage is that you have to know where and how to find that information quickly in an unfamiliar text. This makes it easy to fall for one of the incorrect answer choices, especially since they are designed to mislead you.

The best way to do your best on this passage/question format is to be very familiar with the kinds of questions that are typically asked on the test. Questions most frequently ask you to:

- identify a specific **fact or detail** in the passage
- note the **main idea** of the passage
- make an **inference** based on the passage
- define a **vocabulary** word from the passage

To succeed on a reading comprehension test, you need to know exactly what each of these questions is asking. **Facts and details** are the specific pieces of information that support the passage's main idea. The **main idea** is the thought, opinion, or attitude that governs the whole passage. Generally speaking, facts and details are indisputable—things that don't need to be proven, like statistics (18 million people) or descriptions (a green overcoat). Let's say, for example, you read a sentence that says, *"After the department's reorganization, workers were 50% more productive."* A sentence like this, which gives you the fact that 50% of workers were more productive, might support a main idea that says, *"Every department should be reorganized."* Notice that this main idea is not something indisputable; it is an opinion. The writer thinks all departments should be reorganized, and because this is his opinion (and not everyone shares it), he needs to support his opinion with facts and details.

An **inference**, on the other hand, is a conclusion that can be drawn based on fact or evidence. For example, you can infer—based on the fact that workers became 50% more productive after the reorganization, which is a dramatic change—that the department had not been efficiently organized. The fact sentence, *"After the department's reorganization, workers were 50% more productive,"* also implies that the reorganization of the department was the reason workers became more productive. There may, of course, have been other reasons, but we can infer only one from this sentence.

As you might expect, **vocabulary** questions ask you to determine the meaning of particular words. Often, if you've read carefully, you can determine the meaning of such words from their context, that is, how the word is used in the sentence or paragraph.

Practice Passage 1: Using the Four Question Types

The following is a sample test passage, followed by four questions. Read the passage carefully, and then answer the questions, based on your reading of the text, by selecting your choice. Then refer to the previous list and note under your answer which type of question has been asked. Correct answers appear immediately after the questions.

In the last decade, community policing has been frequently touted as the best way to reform urban law enforcement. The idea of putting more officers on foot patrol in high crime areas, where relations with police have frequently been strained, was initiated in Houston in 1983 under the leadership of then-Commissioner Lee Brown. He believed that officers should be accessible to the community at the street level. If officers were assigned to the same area over a period of time, those officers would eventually build a network of trust with neighborhood residents. That trust would mean that merchants and residents in the community would let officers know about criminal activities in the area and would support police intervention. Since then, many large cities have experimented with Community-Oriented Policing (COP) with mixed results. Some have found that police and citizens are grateful for the opportunity to work together. Others have found that unrealistic expectations by citizens and resistance from officers have combined to hinder the effectiveness of COP. It seems possible, therefore, that a good idea may need improvement before it can truly be considered a reform.

1. Community policing has been used in law enforcement since

   a. the late 1970s.

   b. the early 1980s.

   c. the Carter administration.

   d. Lee Brown was New York City Police Commissioner.

   Question type _____

2. The phrase *a network of trust* in this passage suggests that

   a. police officers can rely only on each other for support.

   b. community members rely on the police to protect them.

   c. police and community members rely on each other.

   d. community members trust only each other.

   Question type _____

3. The best title for this passage would be

   a. Community Policing: The Solution to the Drug Problem.

   b. Houston Sets the Pace in Community Policing.

   c. Communities and Cops: Partners for Peace.

   d. Community Policing: An Uncertain Future?

   Question type _____

4. The word *touted* in the first sentence of the passage most nearly means

   a. praised.

   b. denied.

   c. exposed.

   d. criticized.

   Question type _____

Answers and Explanations

Don't just look at the right answers and move on. The explanations are the most important part, so read them carefully. Use these explanations to help you understand how to tackle each kind of question the next time you come across it.

1. b. Question type: fact or detail. The passage identifies 1983 as the first large-scale use of community policing in Houston. Don't be misled by trying to figure out when Carter was president. Also, if you happen to know that Lee Brown was New York City's police commissioner, don't let that information lead you away from the information contained in the passage alone. Brown was commissioner in Houston when he initiated community policing.

2. c. Question type: inference. The *network of trust* referred to in this passage is between the community and the police, as you can see from the sentence where the phrase appears. The key phrase in the question is *in this passage.* You may think that police can rely only on each other, or one of the other answer choices may appear equally plausible to you. But, your choice of answers must be limited to the one suggested *in this passage.* Another tip for questions like this: Beware of absolutes! Be suspicious of any answer containing words like *only, always,* or *never.*

3. d. Question type: main idea. The title always expresses the main idea. In this passage, the main idea comes at the end. The sum of all the details in the passage suggests that community policing is not without its critics and that therefore its future is uncertain. Another key phrase is *mixed results,* which means that some communities haven't had full success with community policing.

4. a. Question type: vocabulary. The word *touted* is linked in this passage with the phrase *the best way to reform*. Most people would think that a good way to reform something is praiseworthy. In addition, the next few sentences in the passage describe the benefits of community policing. Criticism of or a negative response to the subject doesn't come until later in the passage.

▶ Detail and Main Idea Questions

Main idea questions and **fact or detail** questions are both asking you for information that's right there in the passage. All you have to do is find it.

Detail or Fact Questions

In detail or fact questions, you have to identify a specific item of information from the text. This is usually the simplest kind of question. You just have to be able to separate important information from less important information. However, the choices may often be very similar, so you must be careful not to get confused.

Be sure you read the passage and questions carefully. In fact, it is usually a good idea to read the questions first, *before* you even read the passage, so you will know what details to look out for.

Main Idea Questions

The main idea of a passage, like that of a paragraph or a book, is what it is *mostly* about. The main idea is like an umbrella that covers all of the ideas and details in the passage, so it is usually something general, not specific. For example, in Practice Passage 1, question 3 asked you what title would be best for the passage, and the correct answer was "Community Policing: An Uncertain Future." This is the best answer because it's the only one that includes both the positive and negative sides of community policing, both of which are discussed in the passage.

Sometimes the main idea is stated clearly, often in the first or last sentence of the passage. The main idea is expressed in the *last* sentence of Practice Passage 1, for example. The sentence that expresses the main idea is often referred to as the **topic sentence**.

At other times, the main idea is not stated in a topic sentence but is *implied* in the overall passage, and you will need to determine the main idea by inference. Because there may be much information in the passage, the trick is to understand what all that information adds up to—the gist of what the author wants you to know. Often some of the wrong answers on main idea questions are specific facts or details from the passage. A good way to test yourself is to ask, "Can this answer serve as a *net* to hold the whole passage together?" If not, chances are you have chosen a fact or detail, not a main idea.

Practice Passage 2: Detail and Main Idea Questions

Practice answering main idea and detail questions by working on the questions that follow this passage. Select the answers to the questions, and then check your answers against the key that appears immediately after the questions.

There are three different kinds of burns: first degree, second degree, and third degree. It is important for firefighters to be able to recognize each of these types of burns so that they can be sure burn victims are given proper medical treatment. The least serious burn is the first-degree burn, which causes the skin to turn red but does not cause blistering. A mild sunburn is a good example of a first-degree burn, and, like a mild sunburn, first-degree burns generally do not require medical treatment other than a gentle cooling of the burned skin with ice or cold tap water.

Second-degree burns, on the other hand, do cause blistering of the skin and should be treated immediately. These burns should be immersed in warm water and then wrapped in a sterile dressing or bandage. (Do not apply butter or grease to these burns; despite the old wives' tale, butter does *not* help burns heal and actually increases chances of infection.) If second-degree burns cover a large part of the body, then the victim should be taken to the hospital immediately for medical care.

Third-degree burns are those that char the skin and turn it black, or burn so deeply that the skin shows white. These burns usually result from direct contact with flames and have a great chance of becoming infected. All third-degree burns should receive immediate hospital care. They should not be immersed in water, and charred clothing should not be removed from the victim. If possible, a sterile dressing or bandage should be applied to burns before the victim is transported to the hospital.

1. Which of the following would be the best title for this passage?
   a. Dealing with Third-Degree Burns
   b. How to Recognize and Treat Different Burns
   c. Burn Categories
   d. Preventing Infection in Burns

2. Second-degree burns should be treated with
   a. butter.
   b. nothing.
   c. cold water.
   d. warm water.

3. First-degree burns turn the skin
   a. red.
   b. blue.
   c. black.
   d. white.

4. Which of the following best expresses the main idea of the passage?
   a. There are three different types of burns.
   b. Firefighters should always have cold compresses on hand.
   c. Different burns require different types of treatment.
   d. Butter is not good for healing burns.

Answers and Explanations

1. **b.** A question that asks you to choose a title for a passage is a main idea question. This main idea is expressed in the second sentence, the topic sentence: *It is important for firefighters to be able to recognize each of these types of burns so that they can be sure burn victims are given proper treatment.* Answer **b** expresses this idea and is the only title that encompasses all of the ideas expressed in the passage. Answer **a** is too limited; it deals only with one of the kinds of burns discussed in the passage. Likewise, answers **c** and **d** are also too limited. Answer **c** covers types of burns but not their treatment, and **d** deals only with preventing infection, which is only a secondary part of the discussion of treatment.

2. **d.** The answer to this fact question is clearly expressed in the sentence, *These burns should be immersed in warm water and then wrapped in a sterile dressing or bandage.* The hard part is keeping track of whether *these burns* refers to the kind of burns in the question, which is second-degree burns. It's easy to choose a wrong answer here because all of the answer choices are mentioned in the passage. You need to read carefully to be sure you match the right burn to the right treatment.

3. a. This is another fact or detail question. The passage says that a first-degree burn *causes the skin to turn red*. Again, it's important to read carefully because all of the answer choices (except **b**, which can be eliminated immediately) are listed elsewhere in the passage.

4. c. Clearly this is a main idea question, and **c** is the only choice that encompasses the whole passage. Answers **b** and **d** are limited to *particular* burns or treatments, and answer **a** discusses only burns and not their treatment. In addition, the second sentence tells us that *it is important for firefighters to be able to recognize each of these types of burns so that they can be sure burn victims are given proper medical treatment.*

▶ Inference and Vocabulary Questions

Questions that ask you about the meaning of vocabulary words in the passage and those that ask what the passage *suggests* or *implies* (inference questions) are different from detail or main idea questions. In **vocabulary** and **inference** questions, you usually have to pull ideas from the passage, sometimes from more than one place.

Inference Questions

Inference questions can be the most difficult to answer because they require you to draw meaning from the text when that meaning is implied rather than directly stated. Inferences are conclusions that we draw based on the clues the writer has given us. When you draw inferences, you have to look for such clues as word choice, tone, and specific details that suggest a certain conclusion, attitude, or point of view. You have to read between the lines in order to make a judgment about what an author was implying in the passage.

A good way to test whether you have drawn an acceptable inference is to ask, "What evidence do I have for this inference?" If you can't find any, you probably have the wrong answer. You need to be sure that your inference is logical and that it is based on something that is suggested or implied in the passage itself—not by what you or others might think. You need to base your conclusions on evidence—facts, details, and other information—not on random hunches or guesses.

Vocabulary Questions

Questions designed to test vocabulary are really trying to measure how well you can figure out the meaning of an unfamiliar word from its context. Context refers to the words and ideas surrounding a vocabulary word. If the context is clear enough, you should be able to substitute a nonsense word for the one being sought, and you would still make the right choice because you could determine meaning strictly from the sense of the sentence.

For example, you should be able to determine the meaning of the italicized nonsense word below based on its context:

The speaker noted that it gave him great *terivinix* to announce the winner of the Outstanding Leadership Award.

In this sentence, *terivinix* most likely means
a. pain.
b. sympathy.
c. pleasure.
d. anxiety.

Clearly, the context of an award makes **c**, *pleasure*, the best choice. Awards don't usually bring pain, sympathy, or anxiety.

When confronted with an unfamiliar word, try substituting a nonsense word and see if the context gives you the clue. If you are familiar with prefixes, suffixes, and word roots, you can also use this knowledge to help you determine the meaning of an unfamiliar word.

You should be careful not to guess at the answer to vocabulary questions based on how you may have seen the word used before or what you *think* it means. Many words have more than one possible meaning, depending on the context in which they are used, and a word you have seen used one way may mean something else in a test passage. Also, if you don't look at the context carefully, you may make the mistake of confusing the vocabulary word with a similar word. For example, the vocabulary word may be *taut* (meaning *tight),* but if you read too quickly or don't check the context, you might think the word is *tout* (meaning *publicize* or *praise)* or *taunt* (meaning *tease).* Always read carefully and be sure that what you think the word means fits into the context of the passage you are being tested on.

Practice Passage 3: Inference and Vocabulary Questions

The questions that follow this passage are strictly vocabulary and inference questions. Select the answers to the questions, and then check your answers against the key that appears immediately after the questions.

Dealing with irritable patients is a great challenge for healthcare workers on every level. It is critical that you do not lose your patience when confronted by such a patient. When handling irate patients, be sure to remember that they are not angry at you; they are simply projecting their anger at something else *onto* you. Remember that if you respond to these patients as irritably as they act with you, you will only increase their hostility, making it much more difficult to give them proper treatment. The best thing to do is to remain calm and ignore any

imprecations patients may hurl your way. Such patients may be irrational and may not realize what they are saying. Often these patients will purposely try to anger you just to get some reaction out of you. If you react to this behavior with anger, they win by getting your attention, but you both lose because the patient is less likely to get proper care.

1. The word *irate* as it is used in the passage most nearly means
   a. irregular, odd.
   b. happy, cheerful.
   c. ill-tempered, angry.
   d. sloppy, lazy.

2. The passage suggests that healthcare workers
   a. easily lose control of their emotions.
   b. are better off not talking to their patients.
   c. must be careful in dealing with irate patients because the patients may sue the hospital.
   d. may provide inadequate treatment if they become angry at patients.

3. An *imprecation* is most likely
   a. an object.
   b. a curse.
   c. a joke.
   d. a medication.

4. Which of the following best expresses the writer's views about irate patients?
   a. Some irate patients just want attention.
   b. Irate patients are always miserable.
   c. Irate patients should be made to wait for treatment.
   d. Managing irate patients is the key to a successful career.

Answers and Explanations

1. **c.** This is a vocabulary question. *Irate* means *ill-tempered, angry.* It should be clear that **b**, *happy, cheerful,* is not the answer; dealing with happy patients is normally not *a great challenge.* Patients that are **a**, *irregular, odd,* or **d**, *sloppy, lazy,* may be a challenge in their own way, but they aren't likely to rouse a healthcare worker to anger. In addition, the passage explains that irate patients are not *angry at you,* and *irate* is used as a synonym for *irritable,* which describes the patients under discussion in the very first sentence.

2. **d.** This is an inference question, as the phrase *the passage suggests* might have told you. The idea that angry healthcare workers might give inadequate treatment is implied by the passage as a whole, which seems to be an attempt to prevent angry reactions to irate patients. Furthermore, the last sentence in particular makes this inference possible: *If you react to this behavior with anger . . . you both lose because the patient is less likely to get proper care.* Answer **c** is not correct, because while it maybe true that some irate patients have sued the hospital in the past, there is no mention of suits anywhere in this passage. Likewise, answer **b** is incorrect; the passage does suggest ignoring patients' insults, but nowhere does it recommend not talking to patients—it simply recommends not talking angrily. And while it may be true that some healthcare workers may lose control of their emotions, the passage does not provide any facts or details to support choice **a,** that they *easily lose control.* Watch out for key words like *easily* that may distort the intent of the passage.

3. **b.** If you didn't know what an *imprecation* is, the context should reveal that it's something you can ignore, so neither choice **a,** an *object,* nor choice **d,** a *medication,* is a likely answer. Furthermore, choice **c** is not likely either, since an irate patient is not likely to be making jokes.

4. **a.** The writer seems to believe that some irate patients just want attention, as is suggested by the sentence, *Often these patients will purposely try to anger you just to get some reaction out of you. If you react to this behavior with anger, they win by getting your attention.* It should be clear that choice **b** cannot be the answer, because it includes an absolute: *Irate patients are always miserable.* Perhaps *some* of the patients are *often* miserable, but an absolute like *always* is almost always wrong. Besides, this passage refers to patients who maybe irate in the hospital, but we have no indication of what these patients are like at other times, and *miserable* and *irate* are not exactly the same thing, either. Answer **c** is also incorrect because the purpose of the passage is to ensure that patients receive *proper treatment* and that irate patients are not discriminated against because of their behavior. Thus, *irate patients should be made to wait for treatment* is not a logical answer. Finally, choice **d** cannot be correct because though it may be true, there is no discussion of career advancement in the passage.

▶ Review: Putting It All Together

A good way to solidify what you have learned about reading comprehension questions is for *you* to write the questions. Here's a passage, followed by space for you to write your own questions. Write one question for each of the four types: fact or detail, main idea, inference, and vocabulary.

The "broken window" theory was originally developed to explain how minor acts of vandalism or disrespect can quickly escalate to crimes and attitudes that break down the entire social fabric of an area. It is a theory that can easily be applied to any situation in society. The theory contends that if a broken window in an abandoned building is not replaced quickly, soon all the windows will be broken. In other words, a small violation, if condoned, leads others to commit similar or greater violations. Thus, after all the windows have been broken, the building is likely to be looted and perhaps even burned down. According to this theory, violations increase exponentially. Thus, if disrespect to a superior is tolerated, others will be tempted to be disrespectful as well. A management crisis could erupt literally overnight. For example, if one firefighter begins to disregard proper housewatch procedure by neglecting to keep up the housewatch administrative journal, and this firefighter is not reprimanded, others will follow suit by committing similar violations of procedure, thinking, "If he can get away with it, why can't I?" So what starts out as a small thing, a violation that may seem not to warrant disciplinary action, may actually ruin the efficiency of the entire firehouse, putting the people the firehouse serves at risk.

1. Fact or Detail question: _____

_____

   a.

   b.

   c.

   d.

2. Main idea question: _____

_____

   a.

   b.

   c.

   d.

3. Inference question: _____

_____

   a.

   b.

   c.

   d.

4. Vocabulary question: _____

_____

   a.

   b.

   c.

   d.

Possible Questions

Here is one question of each type based on the previous passage. Your questions may be very different, but these will give you an idea of the kinds of questions that could be asked.

1. Detail question: According to the passage, which of the following could happen "overnight"?
   a. The building will be burned down.
   b. The firehouse may become unmanageable.
   c. A management crisis might erupt.
   d. The windows will all be broken.

2. Main idea question: Which of the following best expresses the main idea of the passage?
   a. Even minor infractions warrant disciplinary action.
   b. Broken windows must be repaired immediately.
   c. People shouldn't be disrespectful to their superiors.
   d. Housewatch must be taken seriously.

3. Inference question: The passage suggests that
   a. the broken window theory is inadequate.
   b. managers need to know how to handle a crisis.
   c. firefighters are lazy.
   d. people will get away with as much as they can.

4. Vocabulary question: In this passage, *condoned* most nearly means
   a. punished.
   b. overlooked.
   c. condemned.
   d. applauded.

Answers

1. c.
2. a.
3. d.
4. b.

▶ Additional Resources

Here are two other ways you can build the vocabulary and knowledge that will help you do well on reading comprehension questions.

- Practice asking the four sample question types about passages you read for information or pleasure.
- Use your library. Many public libraries have sections that contain materials for adult learners. In these sections you can find books with exercises in reading and study skills. It's also a good idea to enlarge your base of information by reading related books and articles. Most libraries have computer systems that allow you to access information quickly and easily. Library personnel will show you how to use the computers and other equipment.

If English Isn't Your First Language

When non-native speakers of English have trouble with reading comprehension tests, it's often because they lack the cultural, linguistic, and historical frame of reference that native speakers enjoy. People who have not lived in or been educated in the United States often don't have the background information that comes from growing up reading American newspapers, magazines, and textbooks.

A second problem for non-native English speakers is the difficulty in recognizing vocabulary and idioms (expressions like "chewing the fat") that assist comprehension. In order to read with good understanding, it's important to have an immediate grasp of as many words as possible in the text. Test takers need to be able to recognize vocabulary and idioms immediately so that the ideas those words express are clear.

The Long View

Read newspapers, magazines, and other periodicals that deal with current events and matters of local, state, and national importance. Pay special attention to articles related to the career you want to pursue.

Be alert to new or unfamiliar vocabulary or terms that occur frequently in the popular press. Use a highlighter pen to mark new or unfamiliar words as you read. Keep a list of those words and their definitions. Review them for 15 minutes each day. Though at first you may find yourself looking up a lot of words, don't be frustrated—you'll look up fewer and fewer as your vocabulary expands.

During the Test

When you are taking the test, make a picture in your mind of the situation being described in the passage. Ask yourself, "What did the writer mostly want me to think about this subject?"

Locate and underline the topic sentence that carries the main idea of the passage. Remember that the topic sentence—if there is one—may not always be the first sentence. If there doesn't seem to be one, try to determine what idea summarizes the whole passage.

Reading Practice

CHAPTER SUMMARY

This chapter provides more instruction on reading and gives you further opportunity for practice with Paragraph Comprehension questions.

Being able to correctly answer Paragraph Comprehension questions on the ASVAB requires much more than simply knowing what the words mean. This chapter will help you improve your reading ability, focusing on three of the most important things you have to do when reading during the test or on the job:

- understanding the basic facts
- finding the main idea
- making inferences or drawing conclusions

Accomplishing these tasks starts with active reading.

▶ Active Reading

Perhaps the most important thing you can do to build your reading skills is become an *active reader*. Active readers generally do two things when they read:

1. They mark up the text.
2. They make specific observations about the text.

Marking Up the Text

Marking the text actively engages you with the words and ideas you are reading. Marking up the text includes three specific strategies:

- Underlining key words and ideas
- Circling and defining any unfamiliar words or phrases
- Recording your reactions and questions in the margins

When you **underline key words and ideas**, you highlight the most important parts of the text you are reading. You also make it easier to summarize and remember the key points.

Circling unfamiliar vocabulary words is important, too, because a key word or phrase could change the meaning of an entire passage. As an active reader, make sure you look up unknown words immediately. If no dictionary is available, try to determine the meaning of the word as best you can from the surrounding sentences (the *context*).

Finally, **recording your reactions and questions in the margins** turns you from a passive receiver of information into an active learner. You will be much more likely to profit from the ideas and information you read about if you create a "conversation" with the writer in this way.

Of course, if this or any other book you read comes from the library, it's only polite to avoid marking in the book itself. Other readers may have other reactions to record. If the book you are reading belongs to someone else, mark key points on a piece of paper instead.

Making Observations

Good readers know that writers use many different strategies to express their ideas. Even if you know very little about writing strategies, you can make useful observations about what you read that will help you better understand the author's ideas. You can notice, for example, the author's choice of words; the structure of sentences and paragraphs; any repetition of words or ideas; important details about people, places, and things; and so on.

This step—making observations—is essential because our observations are what lead us to logical *inferences* about what we read. Inferences are conclusions based on reason, fact, or evidence. When we misunderstand what we read, it is often because we haven't looked closely enough at the text, and so we base our inferences on our own ideas, not on what's actually written in the text. We end up forcing our own ideas on the author rather than listening to what the author has to say and *then* forming our own ideas about it.

▶ Finding the Facts

As a reader faced with a text, you must get the basic facts: the who, what, when, where, how, and why. What does this piece of writing tell you? What happens? To whom? When, where, how, and why? If you can answer these basic questions, you are on your way to really comprehending what you read.

Let's start with a definition. A fact is:

- something that we know for certain to have happened
- something that we know for certain to be true
- something that we know for certain to exist

Much of what you read is designed to provide you with facts. You may read, for example, about a new office procedure that you must follow; about how the new computer system works; about what happened at the staff meeting. If you are taking a standardized test to help you get a job, you will probably have to answer reading comprehension questions that ask you about the facts in a passage you read. It is very important, therefore, for you to be able to read through these materials and understand the information they convey. What facts are you expected to know? What are you to learn or be aware of? What happened? What is true? What exists?

Fact-Finding Practice 1

Jump right into the task of finding facts. The brief passage that follows is similar to something you might see in a newspaper. Read the passage carefully, and then answer the questions. Remember, careful reading is active reading, so mark up the text as you go. Underline key words and ideas; circle and define any unfamiliar words or phrases; record your reactions and questions in the margins.

On Tuesday, August 30, Mr. Blank, a prominent local citizen, arrived home from work to find his apartment had been robbed. The thieves somehow managed to slip past building security at 131 West Elm Street with nearly all of Mr. Blank's belongings. In fact, the thieves left behind nothing but a stack of old *Home Decorator* magazines and a can of

pork and beans. The robbery was reported by Mr. Blank's neighbor, who found Mr. Blank unconscious in his doorway. Apparently Mr. Blank was so shocked by the robbery that he fainted. His neighbor immediately called an ambulance and then the police. Mr. Blank is now staying with relatives and is offering a reward of $25,000 for any information leading to the arrest of the thieves.

1. What happened to Mr. Blank?

2. When did it happen?

3. Where did it happen?

4. How did Mr. Blank react?

5. Who called the police?

6. What was left in the apartment?

Remember, good reading is active reading. Did you mark up the passage? If so, it may have looked something like this:

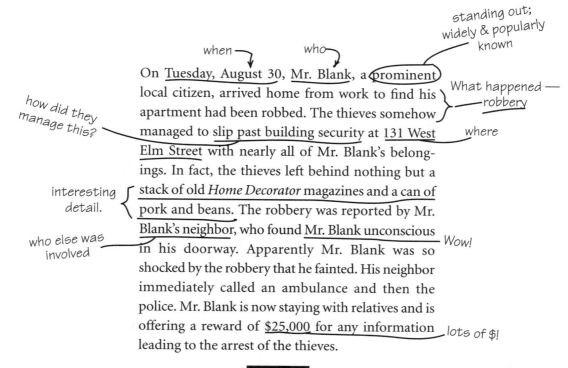

You will notice that the answers to the questions have all been underlined, because these are the key words and ideas in this passage. But here are the answers in a more conventional form:

1. What happened to Mr. Blank? *His apartment was robbed.*

2. When did it happen? *sometime while Mr. Blank was at work on Tuesday, August 30*

3. Where did it happen? *131 West Elm Street*

4. How did Mr. Blank react? *He fainted.*

5. Who called the police? *Mr. Blank's neighbor*

6. What was left in the apartment? *some old* Home Decorator *magazines and a can of pork and beans*

Notice that these questions went beyond the basic who, what, when, and where to include some of the details, like what was left in the apartment. This is because details in reading comprehension can be very important clues that may help answer the remaining questions: who did it, how, and why.

Fact-Finding Practice 2

Here's another passage, this time something a little more like what you might see at work. Read the passage carefully and answer the questions that follow.

To: All New Employees
From: Human Resources

In order for your first paycheck to be processed, we must have a number of documents completed and in our files. Once these documents are in our hands, you will be entered into our payroll system. These documents include: a completed company application; a W-4 form; an I-9 form; a Confidentiality Agreement, if applicable; an emergency contact sheet; and a copy of your resume. You should be sure all of these documents are filled out within your first week of work. In addition, we will need the following documents from you for your file to be complete: two letters of recommendation from previous employers, a high school and college transcript, and an insurance coverage application. We request that you complete your file within your first month of employment.

7. What papers must new employees have on file? List them below.

8. In your list above, circle the items that employees must have on file in order to get paid.

9. When should these circled items be completed?

10. When must the rest of the file be completed?

11. True or False: Everyone must sign a Confidentiality Agreement.

Before you look at the answers, look at the next page to see how you might have marked up the passage to highlight the important information.

To: All New Employees
From: Human Resources

In order for your first paycheck to be processed, we must have a number of documents completed and in our files. Once these documents are in our hands, you will be entered into our payroll system. These documents include: [a completed company application; a W-4 form; an I-9 form; a Confidentiality Agreement, if applicable; an emergency contact sheet; and a copy of your resume.] You should be sure all of these documents are filled out <u>within your first week of work</u>. In addition, we will need the following documents from you for your file to be complete: [two letters of recommendation from previous employers, a high school and college transcript and an insurance coverage application.] We request that you complete your file within your <u>first month of employment</u>.

Important deadline!

Official copy of student's educational record

Documents I need in order to get paid

Documents I need to complete file

Deadline for completing file

With a marked-up text like this, it's very easy to find the answers.

7. What papers must new employees have on file?

(Company application)

(W-4 form)

(I-9 form)

(Confidentiality Agreement (if applicable))

(Emergency contact sheet)

(Resume)

Two letters of recommendation

High school and college transcripts

Insurance coverage application

8. In the previous list, the items that employees must have on file in order to get paid are circled.

9. When should these circled items be completed? *within the employee's first week of work*

10. When must the rest of the file be completed? *within the employee's first month of work*

11. True or False: Everyone must sign a Confidentiality Agreement. *False; only those for whom it is "applicable."*

Fact-Finding Practice 3

Now look at one more short passage. Again, read carefully and then answer the questions that follow.

Today's postal service is more efficient and reliable than ever before. Mail that used to take months to move by horse and by foot now moves around the country in days or hours by truck, train, and plane. First-class mail usually moves from New York City to Los Angeles in three days or less. If your letter or package is urgent, the U.S. Postal Service offers Priority Mail and Express Mail services. Priority Mail is guaranteed to go anywhere in the United States in two days or less. Express Mail will get your package there overnight.

12. Who or what is this passage about?

13. How was mail transported in the past?

14. How is mail transported now?

15. How long does first class mail take?

16. How long does Priority Mail take?

17. How long does Express Mail take?

Once again, here's how you might have marked up this passage:

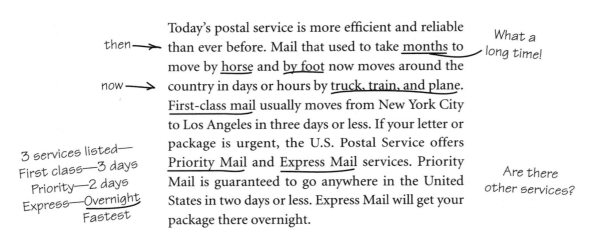

You can see how marking up a text helps make it easier to understand the information a passage conveys.

12. Who or what is this passage about?
the U.S. Postal Service

13. How was mail transported in the past?
by horse and foot

14. How is mail transported now?
by truck, train, and plane

15. How long does first-class mail take?
three days or less

16. How long does Priority Mail take?
two days or less

17. How long does Express Mail take? *overnight*

Active reading is the first essential step to comprehension. Why? Because active reading forces you to really *see* what you are reading, to look closely at what's there. If you look carefully and ask the right questions (who, what, when, where, how, and why), you are on your way to really comprehending what you read.

► Finding the Main Idea

When the previous section talked about establishing the facts—the who, what, when, where, and how—it omitted one very important question: Why? Now you are ready to tackle that question.

All writing is communication: A writer writes to convey his or her thoughts to an audience (the reader—you). Just as you have something to say when you pick up the phone to call someone, writers have something to say when they pick up a pen or pencil to write. The reader might ask, "Why did the author write this? What idea is he or she trying to convey?" What you are really asking is, "What is the writer's main idea?"

Finding the main idea is much like finding the *why*. It usually determines the other factors (the *who, what, when, where,* and *how*). Similarly, in writing, the main idea also determines the *who, what, when,* and *where* the writer will write about, as well as *how* he or she will write.

Subject vs. Main Idea

There's a difference between the *subject* of a piece of writing and its *main idea*. To see the difference, look again at the passage about the postal system.

> Today's postal service is more efficient and reliable than ever before. Mail that used to take months to move by horse and by foot now moves around the country in days or hours by truck, train, and plane. First-class mail usually moves from New York City to Los Angeles in three days or less. If your letter or package is urgent, the U.S. Postal Service offers Priority Mail and Express Mail services. Priority Mail is guaranteed to go anywhere in the United States in two days or less. Express Mail will get your package there overnight.

You will often see a question in the reading comprehension portion of a test that asks, in essence, "What is the main idea of this passage?"

For this passage, you might be tempted to answer: "The post office."

But you would be wrong.

This passage is *about* the post office, yes—but "the post office" is not the main idea of the passage. The post office is merely the *subject* of the passage (*who* or *what* the passage is about). The main idea must say something *about* this subject. The main idea of a text is usually an *assertion* about the subject. An assertion is a statement that requires evidence ("proof") to be accepted as true.

The main idea of a passage is an assertion about its subject, but it is also something more: It is the idea that also holds together or controls the passage. The other sentences and ideas in the passage will all relate to that main idea and serve as evidence that the assertion is true. You might think of the main idea as a net that is cast over the other sentences. The main idea must be general enough to hold all of these ideas together.

Thus, the main idea of a passage is:

- an assertion about the subject
- the general idea that controls or holds together the paragraph or passage

Look at the postal service paragraph once more. You know what the subject is: the post office. Now, see if you can determine the main idea. Read the passage again and look for the idea that makes an assertion about the postal service *and* holds together or controls the whole paragraph. Then answer the following question.

18. Which of the following sentences best summarizes the main idea of the passage?
   a. Express Mail is a good way to send urgent mail.
   b. Mail service today is more effective and dependable.
   c. First-class mail usually takes three days or less.
   d. Priority Mail is a quick alternative to first-class mail.

Because **a** is specific—it tells us *only* about Express Mail—it cannot be the main idea. It does not encompass the rest of the sentences in the paragraph—it doesn't cover Priority Mail or first-class mail. Answers **c** and **d** are also very specific. They tell us only about first-class mail and Priority Mail, so they, too, cannot be the main idea.

But **b**—*Mail service today is more effective and dependable*—is general enough to encompass the whole passage. And the rest of the sentences *support* the idea that this sentence asserts: Each sentence offers proof that the postal service today is indeed more efficient and reliable. Thus, the writer's motive is to tell us about the efficiency and reliability of today's postal service.

Topic Sentences

You will notice that in the paragraph about the postal service, the main idea is expressed clearly in the first sentence: *Today's postal service is more efficient and reliable than ever before.* A sentence such as this one, that clearly expresses the main idea of a paragraph or passage, is often called a **topic sentence**.

In many cases, like the postal service paragraph, you will find the topic sentence at the beginning of the paragraph. You will also frequently find it at the end. Less often, but on occasion, the topic sentence may be found in the middle of the passage. Whatever the case may be, the topic sentence—like *Today's postal service is more efficient and reliable than ever before*—is an assertion, and it needs proof. The proof is found in the facts and ideas that make up the rest of the passage. (Not all passages provide such a clear topic sentence that states the main idea. Such passages will come up later in this chapter.)

Remember that a topic sentence is a clear statement of the main idea of a passage; it must be general enough to encompass all of the ideas in that passage, and it usually makes an assertion about the subject of that passage. Knowing all that, you can answer the following question even without reading a passage.

Topic Sentence Practice 1

19. Which of the following sentences is general enough to be a topic sentence?
a. Java is a computer language.
b. There are many different computer languages.
c. An old computer language is BASIC.
d. Most PCs run Microsoft programs.

The answer is **b**, *There are many different computer languages.* Answers **a**, **c**, and **d** are all specific examples of what is said in **b**, so they are not general enough to be topic sentences.

Topic Sentence Practice 2

Now look at the following paragraph. Underline the sentence that expresses the main idea, and notice how the other sentences work to support that main idea.

Erik always played cops and robbers when he was a boy; now, he's a police officer. Preeti always played school as a little girl; today, she is a high school math teacher. Kara always played store; today, she owns a chain of retail clothing shops. Long before they are faced with the question, "What do you want to be when you grow up?" some lucky people know exactly what they want to do with their lives.

Which sentence did you underline? You should have underlined the *last* sentence: *Long before they are faced with that question "What do you want to be when you grow up?" some lucky people know exactly what they want to do with their lives.* This sentence is a good topic sentence; it expresses the idea that holds together the whole paragraph. The first three sentences—about Erik, Preeti, and Kara—are *specific examples* of these lucky people. Notice that this time the topic sentence is found at the *end* of the paragraph.

Topic Sentence Practice 3

Among the eight sentences below are *two* topic sentences. The other sentences are supporting sentences. Circle the two topic sentences. Then write the numbers of the supporting sentences that go with each topic sentence.

1. Furthermore, government employees receive terrific heathcare coverage.
2. Some police officer duties, like writing reports, have no risk at all.
3. For example, government employees have more paid holidays than employees of private companies.
4. Not all police duties are dangerous.
5. Others, like traffic duty, put police officers at very little risk.
6. Government employees enjoy numerous benefits.
7. Still other duties, like investigating accidents, leave officers free of danger.
8. In addition, government employees are well compensated for overtime hours.

Sentences **4** and **6** are the two topic sentences because both make an assertion about a general subject. The supporting sentences for topic sentence **4**, *Not all police duties are dangerous*, are sentences **2**, **5**, and **7**. The supporting sentences for topic sentence **6**, *Government employees enjoy numerous benefits*, are the remaining sentences: **1**, **3**, and **8**.

Here's how they look as paragraphs:

Not all police duties are dangerous. Some duties, like writing reports, have no risk at all. Others, like traffic duty, offer very little risk. Still other duties, like investigating accidents, leave officers free of danger.

Government employees enjoy numerous benefits. For example, they have more paid holidays than employees of private companies. In addition, they are well compensated for overtime hours. Furthermore, they receive terrific healthcare coverage.

You might have noticed the supporting sentences in the first paragraph about police duties begin with the following words: *some, others*, and *still other*. These words are often used to introduce examples. The second paragraph uses different words, but they have the same function: *for example, in addition*, and *furthermore*. If a sentence begins with such a word or phrase, that is a good indication it is *not* a topic sentence—because it is providing a specific example.

Here are some words and phrases often used to introduce specific examples:

for example	in particular
for instance	some
in addition	others
furthermore	

If you are having trouble finding the main idea of a paragraph, you might try eliminating the sentences that you know contain supporting evidence.

Now you can answer the last of the questions—the *why*. What's the main idea the author wants to convey? By finding the sentence that makes an assertion about the subject of the paragraph and that encompasses the other sentences in the paragraph, you can uncover the author's motive.

▶ Drawing Conclusions

Writers know that they can get an idea across to their readers without directly saying it. Instead of providing a topic sentence that expresses their main idea, many times they simply omit that sentence and instead provide a series of clues through structure and language to get their ideas across.

Finding an **implied main idea** is much like finding a stated main idea. Remember, a main idea is an assertion about the subject that controls or holds together all of the ideas in the passage. If the writer provides a topic sentence that states the main idea, finding the main idea is something of a process of elimination:

You eliminate the sentences that aren't general enough to encompass the whole passage. But what do you do when there is no topic sentence?

You use your observations to make an **inference**— an inference about the main idea or point of the passage.

Finding an implied main idea requires you to use your observations to make an inference that, like a topic sentence, encompasses the whole passage. It might take a little work, but you can make observations that will enable you to find main ideas even when they are not explicitly stated.

Inference Practice 1

For the first example of finding an implied main idea, let's return to our friend Mr. Blank. If you remember, earlier in this chapter, his apartment was robbed. Now look at a statement from the building manager in response to news of the robbery:

This is the third robbery in our building this month. Each time, the thieves have gotten past building security with almost the entire contents of the victim's apartment. Yet each time, the security officers say they have seen nothing unusual.

Now, there is no topic sentence in this paragraph, but you should be able to determine the manager's main idea from the facts he provides and from his tone. What is he suggesting?

20. Which of the following best summarizes the manager's main idea?
   a. There are too many robberies in the building.
   b. There are not enough security officers in the building.
   c. There is something wrong with the security in the building.
   d. The burglars live in the neighborhood.

The correct answer is **c**, *There is something wrong with the security in the building.* How can you tell that this is the main idea? For one thing, it's the only one of the three choices that is general enough to serve as a net for the paragraph; choice **a** is implied only in the first sentence and choices **b** and **d** aren't mentioned at all. In addition, each sentence on its own except for **d** suggests that security in the building has not been working properly. Furthermore, the word *yet* indicates that there is a conflict between the events that have taken place and the duties of the security officers.

Inference Practice 2

Now examine the following statement from Mr. Blank's neighbor, who was also interviewed after the robbery:

Well, Mr. Blank's a pretty carefree man. A few times I've knocked on his door and he just hollers "Come in." I just have to push the door open because it isn't locked. He often forgets things, too, like where he parked his car or where he put his keys. Speaking of his car, he never locks the doors. I'm surprised it has never been stolen. Anyway, one time I found him in the hall searching through his bags because he couldn't find his keys, and it turned out the door was open anyway. Sometimes I wonder how he remembers to eat, let alone to take care of his apartment.

21. What is Mr. Blank's neighbor suggesting?
   a. Mr. Blank forgets everything.
   b. Mr. Blank may have left his door open that day.
   c. Mr. Blank is too carefree for his own good.
   d. Mr. Blank locks his car doors.

You can attack the question this way: Which of these three statements do the sentences in the neighbor's statement support? Try a process of elimination. Do all of the sentences support choice **a**? If not, cross **a** out. Do all of the sentences support choice **b**? Choices **c** or **d**?

The correct answer is **b**, *Mr. Blank may have left his door open that day*. How can you tell? Because this is the only idea that all of the sentences in the neighbor's statement support. You know that Mr. Blank often doesn't lock his door when he's home; you also know that he often forgets things. Thus, the neighbor's statement contains **a**, **c**, and **d**, but none of these can be the main idea because the neighbor discusses all three things in combination. This combination makes it likely that Mr. Blank left his apartment door open on the day he was robbed.

Inference Practice 3

Now look at a paragraph in which the *language* the writer uses is what enables you to determine meaning. Read the following paragraph carefully and see if you can determine the implied main idea of the paragraph.

Mr. B, my manager, is six feet ten inches tall with eyes that pierce like knives. He invades the office at precisely 8:00 A.M. every morning demanding this report and that report. He spends half of the day looking over my shoulder and barking orders. And whenever there's a mistake—even if it's his fault— he blames it on me.

Before you decide on the implied main idea, list your observations. What did you notice about the language in this paragraph? An example is provided to get you started.

Observations

Example: I noticed that Mr. B's eyes are compared to knives.

22. Which of the following best expresses the implied message of the passage?
   a. Working for Mr. B is a challenge.
   b. Working for Mr. B is like working for a tyrant.
   c. Mr. B is a terrible manager.
   d. Mr. B has an abrasive personality.

The correct answer is **b**, *working for Mr. B is like working for a tyrant*. There are many clues in the language of this paragraph that lead you to this inference. First, you probably noticed that Mr. B *has eyes that pierce like knives*. This comparison (called a *simile*) suggests that Mr. B does not look at others very warmly; instead, his eyes stab.

Second, the author tells us that Mr. B *invades the office at precisely 8:00 A.M. every morning. Invade* is a key word choice. The author could have said that Mr. B *storms into* the office or *barges into* the office, but he chose the word *invades*, as if Mr. B doesn't belong there or as if Mr. B is attempting to take over territory that isn't his. Furthermore, Mr. B spends the day *barking orders*, and, like a tyrant, he passes the blame onto others when something goes wrong. Thus, though answers **a**, **c**, and **d** may be true, answer **b** is the only idea that all of the sentences in the paragraph support.

Of course, this person's description of Mr. B is very subjective, using as it does the first person point of view. As an active reader, you should wonder whether everyone sees Mr. B this way or if this employee is unable to be objective about Mr. B.

Many writers use implication to convey meaning rather than directly stating their ideas. Finding the implied main idea requires a little detective work, but it is not as difficult as you may have thought.

► Tips for Continuing to Improve Your Reading

Reading is like exercise: If you don't keep doing it, you will get out of shape. Like muscles that grow stronger and bigger with each repetition, your reading skills will grow stronger with each text that you read.

The following are some ways you can continue to strengthen your reading comprehension skills:

- **Read!** Read anything—books, newspapers, magazines, novels, poems. The more you read, the better. Set yourself a reading goal: one book a month, two books while you are on vacation, a half hour of reading every night before bed.
- **Discover new authors.** Check out the bestseller list and try one of the books on that list. If it's a bestseller, it's probably a book that appeals to a wide variety of readers, and chances are good that you will like it.
- **Spend some time in bookstores.** There are bound to be books and authors out there that appeal to some of your interests. Don't be afraid to ask a salesperson to help you. Describe your interests and your preferences in style, and he or she can help you find books you will enjoy reading.
- **Take a course at a local college.** Most courses (other than mathematics and computer science) require a significant amount of reading, so they are a great way to sharpen your reading comprehension skills while you work towards a degree or greater understanding of a certain subject. In addition, if you are in a class, you will have a teacher who can guide you to make sure you are correctly comprehending what you read.
- **Join a reading group.** Most cities and towns have a club that meets every two weeks or each month to discuss a selected book. In these groups, you will get to discuss your ideas and questions with a group of friends and associates in an informal setting. If your area doesn't have a reading group, start your own. You and your friends can take turns choosing which book you will read and discuss it.

12▶ Practice ASVAB Core Test 2

CHAPTER SUMMARY

Here's another sample ASVAB core for you to practice with. After working through the review and practice material in the previous chapters, take this test to see how much your score has improved.

This practice test will be a good measure of how much you've learned from working through the lessons in this book, especially if you took the first practice test in Chapter 5. As in that test, this test includes four out of the eight subtests that make up the ASVAB. These four subtests count toward your Armed Forces Qualifying Test (AFQT) score, which will determine whether or not you will be allowed to enlist in the military.

For this test, simulate the actual test-taking experience as closely as you can. Find a quiet place to work where you won't be disturbed. Use the answer sheet provided and use a timer or stopwatch to time each section. The times are marked at the beginning of each section.

After the exam, review the answer explanations to understand each question you missed. To find out more about your score, review Chapter 3.

► Part 1: Arithmetic Reasoning

1.	(a)	(b)	(c)	(d)	11.	(a)	(b)	(c)	(d)	21.	(a)	(b)	(c)	(d)
2.	(a)	(b)	(c)	(d)	12.	(a)	(b)	(c)	(d)	22.	(a)	(b)	(c)	(d)
3.	(a)	(b)	(c)	(d)	13.	(a)	(b)	(c)	(d)	23.	(a)	(b)	(c)	(d)
4.	(a)	(b)	(c)	(d)	14.	(a)	(b)	(c)	(d)	24.	(a)	(b)	(c)	(d)
5.	(a)	(b)	(c)	(d)	15.	(a)	(b)	(c)	(d)	25.	(a)	(b)	(c)	(d)
6.	(a)	(b)	(c)	(d)	16.	(a)	(b)	(c)	(d)	26.	(a)	(b)	(c)	(d)
7.	(a)	(b)	(c)	(d)	17.	(a)	(b)	(c)	(d)	27.	(a)	(b)	(c)	(d)
8.	(a)	(b)	(c)	(d)	18.	(a)	(b)	(c)	(d)	28.	(a)	(b)	(c)	(d)
9.	(a)	(b)	(c)	(d)	19.	(a)	(b)	(c)	(d)	29.	(a)	(b)	(c)	(d)
10.	(a)	(b)	(c)	(d)	20.	(a)	(b)	(c)	(d)	30.	(a)	(b)	(c)	(d)

► Part 2: Word Knowledge

1.	(a)	(b)	(c)	(d)	10.	(a)	(b)	(c)	(d)	19.	(a)	(b)	(c)	(d)
2.	(a)	(b)	(c)	(d)	11.	(a)	(b)	(c)	(d)	20.	(a)	(b)	(c)	(d)
3.	(a)	(b)	(c)	(d)	12.	(a)	(b)	(c)	(d)	21.	(a)	(b)	(c)	(d)
4.	(a)	(b)	(c)	(d)	13.	(a)	(b)	(c)	(d)	22.	(a)	(b)	(c)	(d)
5.	(a)	(b)	(c)	(d)	14.	(a)	(b)	(c)	(d)	23.	(a)	(b)	(c)	(d)
6.	(a)	(b)	(c)	(d)	15.	(a)	(b)	(c)	(d)	24.	(a)	(b)	(c)	(d)
7.	(a)	(b)	(c)	(d)	16.	(a)	(b)	(c)	(d)	25.	(a)	(b)	(c)	(d)
8.	(a)	(b)	(c)	(d)	17.	(a)	(b)	(c)	(d)					
9.	(a)	(b)	(c)	(d)	18.	(a)	(b)	(c)	(d)					

► Part 3: Paragraph Comprehension

1.	(a)	(b)	(c)	(d)	6.	(a)	(b)	(c)	(d)	11.	(a)	(b)	(c)	(d)
2.	(a)	(b)	(c)	(d)	7.	(a)	(b)	(c)	(d)	12.	(a)	(b)	(c)	(d)
3.	(a)	(b)	(c)	(d)	8.	(a)	(b)	(c)	(d)	13.	(a)	(b)	(c)	(d)
4.	(a)	(b)	(c)	(d)	9.	(a)	(b)	(c)	(d)	14.	(a)	(b)	(c)	(d)
5.	(a)	(b)	(c)	(d)	10.	(a)	(b)	(c)	(d)	15.	(a)	(b)	(c)	(d)

► Part 4: Mathematics Knowledge

1.	(a)	(b)	(c)	(d)	13.	(a)	(b)	(c)	(d)	25.	(a)	(b)	(c)	(d)
2.	(a)	(b)	(c)	(d)	14.	(a)	(b)	(c)	(d)	26.	(a)	(b)	(c)	(d)
3.	(a)	(b)	(c)	(d)	15.	(a)	(b)	(c)	(d)	27.	(a)	(b)	(c)	(d)
4.	(a)	(b)	(c)	(d)	16.	(a)	(b)	(c)	(d)	28.	(a)	(b)	(c)	(d)
5.	(a)	(b)	(c)	(d)	17.	(a)	(b)	(c)	(d)	29.	(a)	(b)	(c)	(d)
6.	(a)	(b)	(c)	(d)	18.	(a)	(b)	(c)	(d)	30.	(a)	(b)	(c)	(d)
7.	(a)	(b)	(c)	(d)	19.	(a)	(b)	(c)	(d)	31.	(a)	(b)	(c)	(d)
8.	(a)	(b)	(c)	(d)	20.	(a)	(b)	(c)	(d)	32.	(a)	(b)	(c)	(d)
9.	(a)	(b)	(c)	(d)	21.	(a)	(b)	(c)	(d)	33.	(a)	(b)	(c)	(d)
10.	(a)	(b)	(c)	(d)	22.	(a)	(b)	(c)	(d)	34.	(a)	(b)	(c)	(d)
11.	(a)	(b)	(c)	(d)	23.	(a)	(b)	(c)	(d)	35.	(a)	(b)	(c)	(d)
12.	(a)	(b)	(c)	(d)	24.	(a)	(b)	(c)	(d)					

► Part 1: Arithmetic Reasoning

Time: 36 minutes

1. What is the estimated product when 157 and 817 are rounded to the nearest hundred and multiplied?
   a. 160,000
   b. 180,000
   c. 16,000
   d. 80,000

2. A large coffee pot holds 120 cups. It is about two-thirds full. About how many cups are in the pot?
   a. 40 cups
   b. 80 cups
   c. 60 cups
   d. 90 cups

3. Mr. Tupper is purchasing gifts for his family. He stops to consider what else he has to buy. A quick mental inventory of his shopping bag so far reveals the following:

1 cashmere sweater, valued at	$260
3 diamond bracelets, each valued at	$365
1 computer game, valued at	$78
1 cameo brooch, valued at	$130

   Later, having coffee in the Food Court, he suddenly remembers that he has purchased only two diamond bracelets, not three, and that the cashmere sweater was on sale for $245. What is the total value of the gifts Mr. Tupper has purchased so far?
   a. $833
   b. $1,183
   c. $1,198
   d. $1,563

This is a list of ingredients needed to make 16 brownies. Use this list to answer questions 4 and 5.

Deluxe Brownies
$\frac{2}{3}$ cup butter
5 squares (1 ounce each) unsweetened chocolate
$1\frac{1}{2}$ cups sugar
2 teaspoons vanilla
2 eggs
1 cup flour

4. How much sugar is needed to make 8 brownies?
   a. $\frac{3}{4}$ cup
   b. 3 cups
   c. $\frac{2}{3}$ cup
   d. $\frac{5}{8}$ cup

5. What is the greatest number of brownies that can be made if the baker has only one cup of butter?
   a. 12
   b. 16
   c. 24
   d. 32

6. One lap on an outdoor track measures a quarter of a mile around. To run a total of three and a half miles, how many laps must a person complete?
   a. 7
   b. 10
   c. 13
   d. 14

7. The state of Connecticut will pay two-fifths of the cost of a new school building. If the city of New Haven is building a school that will cost a total of $15,500,000. What will the state pay?
a. $3,100,000
b. $7,750,000
c. $6,200,000
d. $4,550,000

8. Body mass index (BMI) is equal to $\frac{\text{weight in kilograms}}{(\text{height in meters})^2}$. A man who weighs 64.8 kilograms has a BMI of 20. How tall is he?
a. 1.8 meters
b. 0.9 meters
c. 2.16 meters
d. 3.24 meters

9. A floor plan is drawn to scale so that $\frac{1}{4}$ inch represents 2 feet. If a hall on the plan is 4 inches long, how long will the actual hall be when it is built?
a. 2 feet
b. 8 feet
c. 16 feet
d. 32 feet

10. Newly hired nurses have to buy duty shoes at the full price of $84.50, but nurses who have served at least a year get a 15% discount. Nurses who have served at least three years get an additional 10% off the discounted price. How much does a nurse who has served at least three years have to pay for shoes?
a. $63.78
b. $64.65
c. $71.83
d. $72.05

11. There are 176 men and 24 women serving in a particular battalion. What percentage of the battalion's force is women?
a. 12%
b. 14%
c. 16%
d. 24%

12. The basal metabolic rate (BMR) is the rate at which our body uses calories. The BMR for a man in his twenties is about 1,700 calories per day. If 204 of those calories should come from protein, about what percent of this man's diet should be protein?
a. 1.2%
b. 8.3%
c. 12%
d. 16%

13. The condition Down's syndrome occurs in about one in 1,500 children when the mothers are in their twenties. About what percent of all children born to mothers in their twenties are likely to have Down's syndrome?
a. 0.0067%
b. 0.67%
c. 6.7%
d. 0.067%

14. If a population of yeast cells grows from 10 to 320 in a period of five hours, what is the rate of growth?
a. It doubles its numbers every hour.
b. It triples its numbers every hour.
c. It doubles its numbers every two hours.
d. It triples its numbers every two hours.

15. How much water must be added to 1 liter of a 5% saline solution to get a 2% saline solution?
 a. 1L
 b. 1.5 L
 c. 2 L
 d. 2.5 L

16. In the first week of his exercise program, John went on a 15-mile hike. The next week, he increased the length of his hike by 20%. How long was his hike in the second week?
 a. 17 miles
 b. 18 miles
 c. 30 miles
 d. 35 miles

17. All of the rooms in a building are rectangular, with 8-foot ceilings. One room is 9 feet wide by 11 feet long. What is the combined area of the four walls, including doors and windows?
 a. 99 square feet
 b. 160 square feet
 c. 320 square feet
 d. 72 square feet

18. What is the volume of a pyramid that has a rectangular base of 10 inches by 12 inches and a height of 10 inches? ($V = \frac{1}{3}lwh$)
 a. 40 cubic inches
 b. 320 cubic inches
 c. 400 cubic inches
 d. 1,200 cubic inches

19. A child has a temperature of 40° C. What is the child's temperature in degrees Fahrenheit? ($F = \frac{9}{5}C + 32$)
 a. 101° F
 b. 102° F
 c. 103° F
 d. 104° F

20. If jogging for one mile uses 150 calories and brisk walking for one mile uses 100 calories, a jogger has to go how many times as far as a walker to use the same number of calories?
 a. $\frac{1}{2}$
 b. $\frac{2}{3}$
 c. $\frac{3}{2}$
 d. 2

21. A dosage of a certain medication is 12 cc per 100 pounds. What is the dosage for a patient who weighs 175 pounds?
 a. 15 cc
 b. 18 cc
 c. 21 cc
 d. 24 cc

22. A hiker walks 40 miles on the first day of a five-day trip. On each day after that, he can walk only half as far as he did the day before. On average, how far does he walk each day?
 a. 10 miles
 b. 15.5 miles
 c. 20 miles
 d. 24 miles

23. A woman drives west at 45 miles per hour. After half an hour, a man starts to follow her. How fast must he drive to catch up to her three hours after he starts?
 a. 52.5 miles per hour
 b. 55 miles per hour
 c. 60 miles per hour
 d. 67.5 miles per hour

24. A family's gas and electricity bill averages $80 a month for seven months of the year and $20 a month the rest of the year. If the family's bills were averaged over the entire year, what would the monthly bill be?
a. $45
b. $50
c. $55
d. $60

25. Jason is six times as old as Kate. In two years, Jason will be twice as old as Kate is then. How old is Jason now?
a. 3 years old
b. 6 years old
c. 9 years old
d. 12 years old

26. During her first three months at college, a student's long distance phone bills are $103.30, $71.60, and $84.00. Her local phone bill is $18.00 each month. What is her average total monthly phone bill?
a. $86.30
b. $92.30
c. $98.30
d. $104.30

27. A car uses 16 gallons of gas to travel 448 miles. How many miles per gallon does the car get?
a. 22 miles per gallon
b. 24 miles per gallon
c. 26 miles per gallon
d. 28 miles per gallon

28. Land in development is selling for $60,000 per acre. If Jack purchases $1\frac{3}{4}$ acres, how much will he pay?
a. $45,000
b. $135,000
c. $105,000
d. $120,000

29. For every dollar Kyra saves, her employer contributes a dime to her savings, with a maximum employer contribution of $10 per month. If Kyra saves $60 in January, $130 in March, and $70 in April, how much will she have in savings at the end of that time?
a. $270
b. $283
c. $286
d. $290

30. Jackie is paid $822.40 twice a month. If she saves $150.00 per paycheck and pays $84.71 on her student loan each month, how much does she have left to spend each month?
a. $1,175.38
b. $1,260.09
c. $1,410.09
d. $1,560.09

▶ Part 2: Word Knowledge

Time: 11 minutes

Select the choice that best matches the underlined word.

1. According to the code of conduct, "Every officer will be <u>accountable</u> for his or her decisions."
a. applauded
b. compensated
c. responsible
d. approached

2. <u>Scrutinize</u> most nearly means
a. vanish.
b. dissect.
c. neglect.
d. weaken.

3. <u>Enumerate</u> most nearly means
   a. pronounce.
   b. count.
   c. explain.
   d. plead.

4. <u>Emulate</u> most nearly means
   a. imitate.
   b. authorize.
   c. fascinate.
   d. punish.

5. The residents of that area were considered to be <u>compliant</u> in regard to the seat belt law.
   a. skeptical
   b. obedient
   c. forgetful
   d. appreciative

6. Following the disturbance, town officials felt the need to <u>augment</u> the laws pertaining to mass demonstrations.
   a. repeal
   b. evaluate
   c. expand
   d. criticize

7. <u>Aversion</u> most nearly means
   a. harmony.
   b. greed.
   c. weariness.
   d. dislike.

8. <u>Validate</u> most nearly means
   a. confirm.
   b. retrieve.
   c. communicate.
   d. appoint.

9. <u>Antagonist</u> most nearly means
   a. comrade.
   b. opponent.
   c. master.
   d. perfectionist.

10. <u>Perseverance</u> most nearly means
   a. unhappiness.
   b. fame.
   c. persistence.
   d. humility.

11. As soon as the details of the affair were released to the media, the newspaper was <u>inundated</u> with calls from a curious public.
   a. provided
   b. bothered
   c. rewarded
   d. flooded

12. <u>Homogeneous</u> most nearly means
   a. alike.
   b. plain.
   c. native.
   d. dissimilar.

13. <u>Ominous</u> most nearly means
   a. ordinary.
   b. gracious.
   c. quarrelsome.
   d. threatening.

14. When people heard that timid Bob had taken up sky-diving, they were <u>incredulous</u>.
   a. fearful
   b. outraged
   c. disbelieving
   d. inconsolable

15. <u>Recluse</u> most nearly means
 a. prophet.
 b. fool.
 c. intellectual.
 d. hermit.

16. The company recruited her because she was <u>proficient</u> in the use of computers.
 a. experienced
 b. unequaled
 c. efficient
 d. skilled

17. <u>Defray</u> most nearly means
 a. pay.
 b. defend.
 c. cheat.
 d. disobey.

18. <u>Placid</u> most nearly means
 a. flabby.
 b. peaceful.
 c. wise.
 d. obedient.

19. The City Council has given <u>tentative</u> approval to the idea of banning smoking from all public buildings.
 a. provisional
 b. ambiguous
 c. wholehearted
 d. unnecessary

20. <u>Vast</u> most nearly means
 a. attentive.
 b. immense.
 c. steady.
 d. slight.

21. <u>Contemptuous</u> most nearly means
 a. respectful.
 b. unique.
 c. scornful.
 d. insecure.

22. Regarding the need for more free coffee and doughnuts, the group's opinion was <u>unanimous</u>.
 a. divided
 b. uniform
 c. adamant
 d. clear-cut

23. <u>Distinct</u> most nearly means
 a. satisfied.
 b. frenzied.
 c. recognizable.
 d. uneasy.

24. Various methods to <u>alleviate</u> the situation were debated.
 a. ease
 b. tolerate
 c. clarify
 d. intensify

25. <u>Enlighten</u> most nearly means
 a. relocate.
 b. confuse.
 c. comply.
 d. teach.

▶ Part 3: Paragraph Comprehension

Time: 13 minutes

Read each passage and answer the questions that follow.

The supervisors have received numerous complaints over the last several weeks about buses on several routes running hot. Drivers are reminded that each route has several check points at which drivers should check the time. If the bus is ahead of schedule, drivers should delay at the check point until it is the proper time to leave.

1. According to the passage, when a bus is "running hot" it means
   a. the engine is over-heating.
   b. the bus is running ahead of schedule.
   c. the air conditioning is not working.
   d. there is no more room for passengers.

2. According to the passage
   a. every bus stop is also a check point.
   b. it is important to keep customer complaints to a minimum.
   c. drivers tend to rush their routes so they can leave work early.
   d. each bus route has several points at which drivers should check the time.

Drivers are responsible for refueling their trucks at the end of each shift. All other routine maintenance is performed by maintenance department personnel, who are also responsible for maintaining service records. If a driver believes a truck is in need of mechanical repair, he or she should fill out the pink Repair Requisition form and turn it in to the shift supervisor.

3. If a truck is due to have the oil changed, it will be done by
   a. maintenance department personnel.
   b. truck drivers.
   c. shift supervisors.
   d. outside contractors.

4. The passage suggests that trucks
   a. are refueled when they have less than half a tank of gas.
   b. have the oil changed every 1,000 miles.
   c. are refueled at the end of every shift.
   d. are in frequent need of repair.

Hazardous waste is defined as any waste designated by the U.S. Environmental Protection Agency as hazardous. If a sanitation worker is unclear whether a particular item is hazardous, he or she should not handle the item but should instead notify the supervisor for directions.

5. Hazardous waste is
   a. anything too dangerous for workers to handle.
   b. picked up by special trucks.
   c. defined by the U.S. Environmental Protection Agency.
   d. not allowed with regular residential garbage.

6. A sanitation worker comes upon a container of cleaning solvent along with the regular garbage in front of a residence. The container does not list the contents of the cleaner. He should
   a. assume the solvent is safe and deposit it in the sanitation truck.
   b. leave a note for the residents, asking them to list the contents.
   c. contact the supervisor for directions.
   d. leave the container on the curb.

Many people hesitate to adopt a retired racing greyhound because they worry that it will be nervous and will need a large space to run. This is a false impression. Greyhounds have naturally sweet, mild dispositions and are sprinters rather than distance runners; they are sufficiently exercised with a few laps around a fenced-in backyard every day. Greyhounds do not make good watchdogs, but they are very good with children, get along well with other dogs (and usually cats as well), and are very affectionate and loyal.

7. According to the passage, adopting a greyhound is a good idea for people who
   a. do not have children.
   b. live in apartments.
   c. do not usually like dogs.
   d. already have another dog or a cat.

8. One drawback of adopting a greyhound is that they
   a. are not good watch dogs.
   b. are very old when they retire from racing.
   c. are very competitive.
   d. need lots of room to run.

One easy way to plan healthy menus is to shop only in the outer aisles of the grocery store. In most supermarkets, fresh fruit and vegetables, dairy, fresh meat, and frozen foods are in the outer aisles. Grains, like pasta, rice, bread, and cereal, are located on the next aisles, the first inner rows. The inside aisles are where you'll find chips and snacks, cookies and pastries, soda pop and drink mixes—foods that nutritionists say should be eaten rarely, if at all. A side benefit of shopping this way is that grocery shopping takes less time.

9. A good title for this article would be
   a. *Why You Should Shop in a Health Food Store*
   b. *How to Complete Your Grocery Shopping in Less Time*
   c. *How to Shop for Healthy Food*
   d. *How to Cook Healthy Food*

10. According to the passage, the best way to shop in the grocery store is to
   a. make a list and stick to it.
   b. stay in the outside aisles.
   c. look for the best prices.
   d. check the newspaper ads each week.

Law enforcement officers often do not like taking time from their regular duties to testify in court, but testimony is an important part of an officer's job. To be good witnesses, officers should keep complete notes detailing any potentially criminal incidents. When on the witness stand, officers may refer to these notes to refresh their memory about particular events. It is also very important for officers to listen carefully to the questions asked by the lawyers and to provide only the information requested.

11. According to the passage, an officer who is testifying in court
   a. will be questioned by the judge.
   b. may refer to his or her notes while on the witness stand.
   c. must do so without pay.
   d. appreciates taking a break from routine assignments.

12. This passage is probably taken from a
   a. memo entitled "Proper Arrest Procedure."
   b. newspaper article.
   c. bestselling novel.
   d. officers' training manual.

13. According to the passage, testifying in court is
  a. an important part of a police officer's job.
  b. difficult, because lawyers try to trick witnesses.
  c. less stressful for police officers than for other witnesses.
  d. a waste of time, because judges usually let criminals off.

In the summer, the northern hemisphere is slanted toward the Sun, making the days longer and warmer than in winter. The first day of summer is called *summer solstice* and is also the longest day of the year. However, June 21 marks the beginning of winter in the southern hemisphere, when that hemisphere is tilted away from the Sun.

14. According to the passage, when it is summer in the northern hemisphere, in the southern hemisphere it is
  a. spring.
  b. summer.
  c. autumn.
  d. winter.

15. It can be inferred from the passage that, in the southern hemisphere, June 21 is the
  a. autumnal equinox.
  b. winter solstice.
  c. vernal equinox.
  d. summer solstice.

▶ Part 4: Mathematics Knowledge

Time: 24 minutes

1. Which of these lines are parallel?

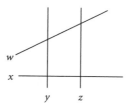

  a. w and x
  b. x and y
  c. x and z
  d. y and z

2. $4\frac{1}{3} + 3\frac{3}{10} =$
  a. $7\frac{2}{15}$
  b. $7\frac{4}{13}$
  c. $7\frac{2}{3}$
  d. $7\frac{19}{30}$

3. $\frac{4}{5}$ is equal to
  a. 0.80.
  b. 0.50.
  c. 0.90.
  d. 0.45.

4. $x(3x^2 + y) =$
  a. $4x^2 + xy$
  b. $4x^2 + x + y$
  c. $3x^3 + 2xy$
  d. $3x^3 + xy$

5. 35% of what number is equal to 14?

   a. 4

   b. 40

   c. 49

   d. 400

6. $\frac{1}{4}$ is equal to

   a. 0.15.

   b. 0.25.

   c. 0.20.

   d. 0.75.

7. If $8n + 25 = 65$, then n is

   a. 5.

   b. 10.

   c. 40.

   d. 90.

8. What is the reciprocal of $3\frac{7}{8}$?

   a. $\frac{31}{8}$

   b. $\frac{8}{31}$

   c. $\frac{8}{21}$

   d. $-\frac{31}{8}$

9. $3\frac{3}{10}$ is equal to

   a. 3.10.

   b. 0.30.

   c. 2.30.

   d. 3.30.

10. Which of these angle measures forms a right triangle?

   a. 45°, 50°, 85°

   b. 40°, 40°, 100°

   c. 40°, 50°, 90°

   d. 20°, 30°, 130°

11. What is another way to write $3\sqrt{12}$?

   a. $12\sqrt{3}$

   b. $6\sqrt{3}$

   c. $2\sqrt{10}$

   d. 18

12. Which is another way to write $\frac{4}{25}$?

   a. 4%

   b. 16%

   c. 40%

   d. 100%

13. What is another way to write 3^4?

   a. 12

   b. 24

   c. 27

   d. 81

14. What is the decimal form of $-1\frac{1}{3}$ rounded to the nearest hundredth?

   a. 1.33

   b. −1.33

   c. 3.67

   d. −3.67

15. $1\frac{3}{4} =$

   a. 1.75

   b. 0.75

   c. 1.34

   d. 1.25

16. Triangles *RST* and *MNO* are similar. What is the length of line segment *MO*?

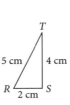 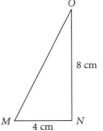

   a. 10 cm

   b. 20 cm

   c. 32 cm

   d. 40 cm

17. Which number sentence is true?

    a. $4.3 < 0.43$

    b. $0.43 < 0.043$

    c. $0.043 > 0.0043$

    d. $0.0043 > 0.43$

18. $0.40 =$

    a. $\frac{1}{4}$

    b. $\frac{1}{5}$

    c. $\frac{2}{5}$

    d. $\frac{3}{4}$

19. Which of these has a 9 in the thousandths place?

    a. 3.0095

    b. 3.0905

    c. 3.9005

    d. 3.0059

20. $0.75 =$

    a. $\frac{1}{4}$

    b. $\frac{1}{5}$

    c. $\frac{2}{7}$

    d. $\frac{3}{4}$

21. Which of the following means $5n + 7 = 17$?

    a. Seven more than 5 times a number is 17.

    b. Five more than 7 times a number is 17.

    c. Seven less than 5 times a number is 17.

    d. Twelve times a number is 17.

22. Lines a, b, and c intersect at point O. Which of these pairs are NOT adjacent angles?

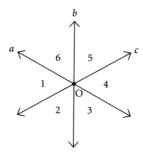

    a. $\angle 1$ and $\angle 6$

    b. $\angle 1$ and $\angle 4$

    c. $\angle 4$ and $\angle 5$

    d. $\angle 2$ and $\angle 3$

23. $2.25 =$

    a. $2\frac{1}{4}$

    b. $2\frac{1}{5}$

    c. $\frac{2}{5}$

    d. $1\frac{3}{4}$

24. What is the value of y when $x = 3$ and $y = 5 + 4x$?

    a. 6

    b. 9

    c. 12

    d. 17

25. 6^3 is equal to

    a. 36.

    b. 1,296.

    c. 18.

    d. 216.

26. What percentage of 50 is 12?

    a. 4%

    b. 14%

    c. 24%

    d. 34%

27. $(14 \times 7) + 12 =$

   a. 98

   b. 266

   c. 110

   d. 100

28. $0.125 =$

   a. $\frac{1}{25}$

   b. $\frac{1}{8}$

   c. $\frac{2}{5}$

   d. $\frac{1}{5}$

29. $3.3 =$

   a. $\frac{3}{33}$

   b. $1\frac{3}{10}$

   c. $3\frac{3}{10}$

   d. $\frac{3}{3}$

30. Which of the following is 14% of 232?

   a. 3.248

   b. 32.48

   c. 16.57

   d. 165.7

31. One side of a square bandage is 4 inches long. What is the perimeter of the bandage?

   a. 4 inches

   b. 8 inches

   c. 12 inches

   d. 16 inches

32. 33 is 12% of which of the following?

   a. 3,960

   b. 396

   c. 275

   d. 2,750

33. The radius of a circle is 13. What is the approximate area of the circle?

   a. 81.64

   b. 530.66

   c. 1,666.27

   d. 169

34. 17^2 is equal to

   a. 34.

   b. 68.

   c. 136.

   d. 289.

35. If the two triangles below are similar, with $\angle A$ equal to $\angle D$, what is the perimeter of $\triangle DEF$?

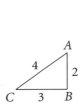
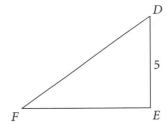

   a. 12

   b. 21

   c. 22.5

   d. 24.75

► Answers

Part 1: Arithmetic Reasoning

1. **a.** 157 is rounded to 200; 817 is rounded to 800; (200)(800) = 160,000.
2. **b.** Multiply 120 by $\frac{2}{3}$. Thus, $\frac{120}{1} \times \frac{2}{3} = \frac{240}{3} = 80$; 120 is written as a fraction with a denominator of 1. The fraction $\frac{240}{3}$ is simplified by dividing 240 by 3 to get 80 cups.
3. **b.** Add the corrected value of the sweater ($245) to the value of the two, not three, bracelets ($730), plus the other two items ($78 and $130).
4. **a.** The recipe is for 16 brownies. Half of that, 8, would reduce the ingredients by half. Half of $1\frac{1}{2}$ cups of sugar is $\frac{3}{4}$ cup.
5. **c.** The recipe for 16 brownies calls for $\frac{2}{3}$ cup butter. An additional $\frac{1}{3}$ cup would make 8 more brownies, for a total of 24 brownies.
6. **d.** To solve this problem, you must convert $3\frac{1}{2}$ to $\frac{7}{2}$ and then divide $\frac{7}{2}$ by $\frac{1}{4}$. The answer, $\frac{28}{2}$, is then reduced to the number 14.
7. **c.** Multiply $15,500,000 by $\frac{2}{5}$; $\frac{15,500,000}{1} \times \frac{2}{5} =$ $6,200,000
8. **a.** Substituting known quantities into the formula yields $20 = \frac{64.8}{x^2}$. Next, you must multiply through by x^2 to get $20x^2 = 64.8$. Now divide through by 20 to get $x^2 = \frac{64.8}{20} = 3.24$. Now take the square root of both sides to get x equals 1.8.
9. **d.** Four inches is equal to 16 quarter inches. Each quarter inch is two feet, so 16 quarter inches is 32 feet.
10. **b.** You can't just take 25% off the original price, because the 10% discount after three years of service is taken off the price that has already been reduced by 15%. Figure the problem in two steps: after the 15% discount the price is $71.83. Ninety percent of that—subtracting 10%—is $64.65.

11. **a.** Add the number of men and women to get the total number: 200. The number of women, 24, is 12% of 200.
12. **c.** The problem is solved by dividing 204 by 1,700. The answer, 0.12, is then converted to a percentage.
13. **d.** The simplest way to solve this problem is to divide 1 by 1,500, which is 0.0006667, and then count off two decimal places to arrive at the percentage, which is 0.06667%. Since the question asks *about what percentage*, the nearest value is 0.067%.
14. **a.** You can use trial and error to arrive at a solution to this problem. After the first hour, the number would be 20, after the second hour 40, after the third hour 80, after the fourth hour 160, and after the fifth hour 320. The other answer choices do not have the same outcome.
15. **b.** Use the equation $.05(1) = .02(x)$, where x is the total amount of water in the resulting 2% solution. Solving for x, you get 2.5. Subtracting the 1 liter of water already present in the 5% solution, you will find that 1.5 liters need to be added.
16. **b.** Twenty percent of 15 miles is 3 miles. Adding 3 to 15 gives 18 miles.
17. **c.** Each 9-foot wall has an area of 9(8) or 72 square feet. There are two such walls, so those two walls combined have an area of 144 square feet. Each 11-foot wall has an area of 11(8) or 88 square feet, and again there are two such walls: 88 (2) = 176. Finally, add 144 and 176 to get 320 square feet.
18. **c.** Using the formula, $V = \frac{1}{3}(10)(12)(10)$.
19. **d.** Substituting 40 for C in the equation yields F $= (\frac{9}{5})(40) + 32 = 72 + 32 = 104$.
20. **b.** $150x = (100)(1)$, where x is the part of a mile a jogger has to go to burn the calories a walker burns in 1 mile. If you divide both

sides of this equation by 150, you get $x = \frac{100}{150}$.
Cancel 50 from both the numerator and
denominator to get $\frac{2}{3}$. This means that a jogger has to jog only $\frac{2}{3}$ of a mile to burn the
same number of calories a walker burns in a
mile of brisk walking.

21. **c.** The ratio is $\frac{12 \text{ cc}}{100 \text{ pounds}} = \frac{x}{175 \text{ pounds}}$ where x is
the number of cc's per 175 pounds. Multiply
both sides by 175 to get $(175)(\frac{12}{100})$ equals x,
so x equals 21.

22. **b.** On the first day, the hiker walks 40 miles. On
the second day, he walks 20 miles. On the
third day, he walks 10 miles. On the fourth
day, he walks 5 miles. On the fifth day, he
walks 2.5 miles. The sum of the miles walked,
then, is 77.5 miles. The average over 5 days is
77.5 divided by 5, or 15.5 miles per day.

23. **a.** The woman will have traveled 3.5 hours at 45
miles per hour for a distance of 157.5 miles.
To reach her in 3 hours, the man must travel
at 157.5 miles per 3 hours, or 52.5 mph.

24. **c.** $80 per month times 7 months is $560. $20
per month times the remaining 5 months is
$100. $560 plus $100 equals $660 for the
entire year. $660 divided by 12 months is $55.

25. **a.** $J = 6K$; $J + 2 = 2(K + 2)$, so $6K + 2 = 2K + 4$,
which means K equals $\frac{1}{2}$. J equals $6K$, or 3.

26. **d.** Add each monthly bill plus $54 for total local
service to get $312.90 for three months.
Dividing by 3 gives an average of $104.30.

27. **d.** 448 miles divided by 16 gallons is 28 miles
per gallon.

28. **c.** Multiply the cost per acre by the number of
acres; $60,000 \times 1\frac{3}{4}$.

29. **b.** Kyra saves $60 + $130 + $70 = $260. In January, her employer contributes $6 and in
April, $7. In March, her employer con-
tributes only $10, the maximum amount.
The total in savings is $260 + $6 + $7 + $10
= $283.

30. **b.** Jackie is paid and saves twice a month, while
she pays her student loan only once a month.

Her monthly salary is $1,644.80. Subtract
$300 in savings and $84.71 for the student
loan to get $1,260.09.

Part 2: Word Knowledge

1. **c.** To be held *accountable* is to be held
responsible.

2. **b.** To *scrutinize* is to examine in detail or *dissect.*

3. **b.** To *enumerate* is to ascertain the number of
or *count.*

4. **a.** To *emulate* a person is to strive to equal that
person or to *imitate* that person.

5. **b.** When one is *compliant,* one is acquiescent
or *obedient.*

6. **c.** To *augment* something is to add to or
expand it.

7. **d.** To have an *aversion* to something is to have a
feeling of repugnance for it or to *dislike* it.

8. **a.** To *validate* something is to *confirm* the
authenticity of it.

9. **b.** To have an *antagonist* is to have an *opponent,*
or one who opposes you.

10. **c.** To have *perseverance* is to be steadfast in your
course or to have *persistence.*

11. **d.** To be *inundated* is to be overwhelmed
or *flooded.*

12. **a.** *Homogeneous* means of the same or a similar
kind, *alike.*

13. **d.** *Ominous* means foreshadowing evil,
threatening.

14. **c.** When one is *incredulous,* one is skeptical
or *disbelieving.*

15. **d.** A *recluse* is a person who lives withdrawn
from the world, a *hermit.*

16. **d.** When one is *proficient* at something, one is
expert or *skilled* at it.

17. **a.** To *defray* is to provide for the payment of
something, to *pay.*

18. **b.** *Placid* means serenely free of disturbance;
calm, *peaceful.*

19. **a.** When something is *tentative,* it is of an
experimental or *provisional* nature.

20. b. Something that is *vast* is huge or *immense.*

21. c. When one is *contemptuous,* one is disdainful or *scornful.*

22. b. When a group's opinion is *unanimous,* it is in accord or *uniform.*

23. c. When something is *distinct,* it is explicit or *recognizable.*

24. a. To *alleviate* something is to make it more bearable or *ease* it.

25. d. To *enlighten* someone is to impart wisdom to that person or to *teach.*

Part 3: Paragraph Comprehension

1. b. The passage explains the procedure for bus drivers to follow when their bus gets ahead of schedule. Therefore, *running hot* means running ahead of schedule.

2. d. The passage indicates that each route contains several check points at which drivers should check the time to see if they are running on schedule.

3. a. The second sentence states that routine maintenance is performed by the maintenance department.

4. c. The first sentence states that drivers are responsible for refueling at the end of each shift; this implies trucks are refueled at the end of every shift.

5. c. According to the passage, hazardous waste is defined by the U.S. Environmental Protection Agency.

6. c. According to the passage, the worker should call his supervisor for directions because he is unclear whether the solvent is unsafe.

7. d. See the last sentence. The passage does not mention choice **b** or choice **c**. Choice **a** is clearly wrong; the passage states the opposite.

8. a. See the last sentence. Choices **b** and **c** are not mentioned, and choice **d** is directly contradicted in the third sentence of the passage.

9. c. This title most nearly captures the main idea of the passage. The other choices either are not mentioned or are secondary ideas in the passage.

10. b. This is the point of the first sentence of the passage.

11. b. The third sentence of the passage states that officers may refer to their notes.

12. d. The passage provides information for law enforcement officers; therefore, it is probably neither a newspaper article or a novel. Choice **a** refers to a memo directed to police officers, but the subject matter is incorrect.

13. a. The first sentence states the importance of officer testimony.

14. d. The first day of summer in the north is the first day of winter in the south.

15. b. The first day of summer is summer solstice; therefore, the first day of winter is winter solstice.

Part 4: Mathematics Knowledge

1. d. The only parallel lines are y and z.

2. d. You must convert both fractions to 30ths before adding.

3. a. Divide 4 by 5 in order to convert the fraction into a decimal; $4 \div 5 = 0.80$.

4. d. $3x$ times x^2 is $3x^3$; x times y is xy.

5. b. Divide 14 by 35 and then multiply the answer by 100 to find the percent.

6. b. Divide 1 by 4 in order to convert the fraction into a decimal. $1 \div 4 = 0.25$.

7. a. The problem is solved by first determining that $8n$ equals 40 and then dividing 40 by 8.

8. b. Convert the mixed number $3\frac{7}{8}$ to the improper fraction $\frac{31}{8}$ and then invert.

9. d. This is a mixed number so it can be broken down into the whole number plus the fraction; $3\frac{3}{10} = 3.0 + \frac{3}{10}$; divide 3 by 10 in order to convert the fraction into a decimal; $3.00 \div 10 = 0.30$. Therefore, $3.0 + 0.30 = 3.30$.

10. **c.** This is the only choice that includes a 90-degree angle.

11. **b.** The square root of 12 is the same as the square root of 4 times 3, which is the same as the square root of 4 times the square root of 3. The square root of 4 is 2. So 3 times the square root of 12 is the same as 3 times 2 times the square root of 3.

12. **b.** Four divided by 25 equals 0.16 or 16%.

13. **d.** $(3)(3)(3)(3) = 81$

14. **b.** $-1\frac{1}{3}$ is a mixed fraction and is equal to the whole number plus the fraction; $-1\frac{1}{3} = -(1 + \frac{1}{3})$. Convert $\frac{1}{3}$ into a decimal by dividing 1 by 3; $1 \div 3 = 0.33\overline{3}$; round this portion of the answer to the nearest hundredth, (two decimal places), to get 0.33; $-(1 + 0.33) = -1.33$.

15. **a.** The mixed number is equal to the whole number plus the fraction; $1\frac{3}{4} = 1.0 + \frac{3}{4}$. Convert the fraction to a decimal by dividing 3 by 4; $3 \div 4 = 0.75$; $1.0 + 0.75 = 1.75$.

16. **a.** The dimensions of $\triangle MNO$ are double those of $\triangle RST$. Line segment RT is 5 cm; therefore line segment MO is 10 cm.

17. **c.** The farther to the right the digits go, the smaller the number.

18. **c.** To convert a decimal into a fraction, first note the number of place positions to the right of the decimal point. In 0.4, the 4 is in the tenths place, which is one place to the right of the decimal point. Therefore, the fraction would be $\frac{4}{10}$. Now, the fraction needs to be reduced to its lowest terms. The number 2 is the greatest common factor of 4 and 10, so divide the numerator and denominator by 2. The final fraction is $\frac{2}{5}$.

19. **a.** In choice **b**, the 9 is in the hundredths place. In choice **c**, it is in the tenths place. In choice **d**, it is in the ten-thousandths place.

20. **d.** In the decimal 0.75, the 75 is two places to the right of the decimal point. Therefore, the fraction would be $\frac{75}{100}$, which can then be reduced by dividing the top and bottom by 25, the greatest common factor of 75 and 100; $\frac{75 \div 25}{100 \div 25} = \frac{3}{4}$.

21. **a.** The expression $5n$ means 5 times n. The addition sign before the 7 indicates the phrase *more than*.

22. **b.** Angles 1 and 4 are the only ones NOT adjacent to each other.

23. **a.** The number 2.25 involves a whole number, which is the 2 to the left of the decimal. This means that the answer will be a mixed number—a whole number plus a fraction. Convert the 0.25 into a fraction; $\frac{25 \div 25}{100 \div 25} = \frac{1}{4}$; adding the whole number, 2, to this fraction gives the answer $2\frac{1}{4}$.

24. **d.** Substitute 3 for x in the expression $5 + 4x$ to determine that y equals 17.

25. **d.** 6^3 is equal to $(6)(6)(6) = 216$.

26. **c.** Divide 12 by 0.5 (50%) to get 24%.

27. **c.** Perform the operation in parentheses first: $(14)(7) = 98$, and then add 12 to get 110.

28. **b.** In the decimal, 0.125 the 125 is three places to the right of the decimal point; 125 is the greatest common factor of 125 and 1,000. The fraction is $\frac{125 \div 125}{1,000 \div 125} = \frac{1}{8}$.

29. **c.** Since there is a number, 3, to the left of the decimal point, this is the whole number; 0.3 is to the right of the decimal point, so this part is the fraction. The 3 is in the tenths place, so the fraction is $\frac{3}{10}$. The final mixed number answer is the whole number (3) plus the fraction ($\frac{3}{10}$); $3 + \frac{3}{10} = 3\frac{3}{10}$.

30. **b.** Convert the percentage to a decimal: $(232)(0.14) = 32.48$.

31. **d.** The perimeter is the total length of all sides. In a square, all four sides are of equal length, so the perimeter is $(4)(4) = 16$.

32. **c.** Divide 33 by 0.12 (12%) to get 275.

33. b. The formula for finding the area of a circle is $A = \pi r^2$. First, square the radius: $(13)(13) = 169$. Then multiply by the approximate value of π, 3.14, to get 530.66.

34. d. 17^2 is equivalent to 17 times 17, which is 289.

35. c. $\overline{DE}$ is 2.5 times greater than $\overline{AB}$; therefore, $\overline{EF}$ is 7.5 and $\overline{DF}$ is 10. Add the three sides together to arrive at the perimeter.

Scoring

Write your raw score (the number you got right) for each test in the blanks below. Then turn to Chapter 3 to find out how to convert these raw scores into the scores the armed services use.

1. Arithmetic Reasoning: _____ right out of 30

2. Word Knowledge: _____ right out of 25

3. Paragraph Comprehension: _____ right out of 15

4. Mathematics Knowledge: _____ right out of 35

Here are the steps you should take, depending on your AFQT score on this practice test:

- **If your AFQT is below 29,** you need more help in reading and/or math. You should spend plenty of time reviewing the lessons and practice questions found in this book.

- **If your AFQT is 29–31,** be sure to focus on your weakest subjects in the review lessons and practice questions that are found in this book.

- **If your AFQT is above 31,** review the areas that give you trouble, and then take the third practice test in Chapter 13 to make sure you are able to get a passing score again.

13▶ Practice ASVAB Core Test 3

CHAPTER SUMMARY

This is the third of three practice battery tests based on the ASVAB core. Take this test for more practice and additional improvement over your score on the first two tests.

Like the previous practice exams, this one contains four out of the eight subtests that make up the ASVAB. These four subtests count toward your Armed Forces Qualifying Test (AFQT) score, which will determine whether or not you will be allowed to enlist in the military.

For this exam, simulate the actual test-taking experience as closely as you can. Work in a quiet place where you won't be interrupted. If you own this book, tear out the answer sheet on page 169 and use your #2 pencils to fill in the circles. Set a timer or stopwatch, and give yourself the appropriate amount of time marked at the beginning of each subtest.

After the exam, use the answer explanations to review the questions you may have missed. Then, use the scoring section at the end of the test and Chapter 3 to see how you did.

▶ Part 1: Arithmetic Reasoning

1.	ⓐ	ⓑ	ⓒ	ⓓ	11.	ⓐ	ⓑ	ⓒ	ⓓ	21.	ⓐ	ⓑ	ⓒ	ⓓ
2.	ⓐ	ⓑ	ⓒ	ⓓ	12.	ⓐ	ⓑ	ⓒ	ⓓ	22.	ⓐ	ⓑ	ⓒ	ⓓ
3.	ⓐ	ⓑ	ⓒ	ⓓ	13.	ⓐ	ⓑ	ⓒ	ⓓ	23.	ⓐ	ⓑ	ⓒ	ⓓ
4.	ⓐ	ⓑ	ⓒ	ⓓ	14.	ⓐ	ⓑ	ⓒ	ⓓ	24.	ⓐ	ⓑ	ⓒ	ⓓ
5.	ⓐ	ⓑ	ⓒ	ⓓ	15.	ⓐ	ⓑ	ⓒ	ⓓ	25.	ⓐ	ⓑ	ⓒ	ⓓ
6.	ⓐ	ⓑ	ⓒ	ⓓ	16.	ⓐ	ⓑ	ⓒ	ⓓ	26.	ⓐ	ⓑ	ⓒ	ⓓ
7.	ⓐ	ⓑ	ⓒ	ⓓ	17.	ⓐ	ⓑ	ⓒ	ⓓ	27.	ⓐ	ⓑ	ⓒ	ⓓ
8.	ⓐ	ⓑ	ⓒ	ⓓ	18.	ⓐ	ⓑ	ⓒ	ⓓ	28.	ⓐ	ⓑ	ⓒ	ⓓ
9.	ⓐ	ⓑ	ⓒ	ⓓ	19.	ⓐ	ⓑ	ⓒ	ⓓ	29.	ⓐ	ⓑ	ⓒ	ⓓ
10.	ⓐ	ⓑ	ⓒ	ⓓ	20.	ⓐ	ⓑ	ⓒ	ⓓ	30.	ⓐ	ⓑ	ⓒ	ⓓ

▶ Part 2: Word Knowledge

1.	ⓐ	ⓑ	ⓒ	ⓓ	10.	ⓐ	ⓑ	ⓒ	ⓓ	19.	ⓐ	ⓑ	ⓒ	ⓓ
2.	ⓐ	ⓑ	ⓒ	ⓓ	11.	ⓐ	ⓑ	ⓒ	ⓓ	20.	ⓐ	ⓑ	ⓒ	ⓓ
3.	ⓐ	ⓑ	ⓒ	ⓓ	12.	ⓐ	ⓑ	ⓒ	ⓓ	21.	ⓐ	ⓑ	ⓒ	ⓓ
4.	ⓐ	ⓑ	ⓒ	ⓓ	13.	ⓐ	ⓑ	ⓒ	ⓓ	22.	ⓐ	ⓑ	ⓒ	ⓓ
5.	ⓐ	ⓑ	ⓒ	ⓓ	14.	ⓐ	ⓑ	ⓒ	ⓓ	23.	ⓐ	ⓑ	ⓒ	ⓓ
6.	ⓐ	ⓑ	ⓒ	ⓓ	15.	ⓐ	ⓑ	ⓒ	ⓓ	24.	ⓐ	ⓑ	ⓒ	ⓓ
7.	ⓐ	ⓑ	ⓒ	ⓓ	16.	ⓐ	ⓑ	ⓒ	ⓓ	25.	ⓐ	ⓑ	ⓒ	ⓓ
8.	ⓐ	ⓑ	ⓒ	ⓓ	17.	ⓐ	ⓑ	ⓒ	ⓓ					
9.	ⓐ	ⓑ	ⓒ	ⓓ	18.	ⓐ	ⓑ	ⓒ	ⓓ					

▶ Part 3: Paragraph Comprehension

1.	ⓐ	ⓑ	ⓒ	ⓓ	6.	ⓐ	ⓑ	ⓒ	ⓓ	11.	ⓐ	ⓑ	ⓒ	ⓓ
2.	ⓐ	ⓑ	ⓒ	ⓓ	7.	ⓐ	ⓑ	ⓒ	ⓓ	12.	ⓐ	ⓑ	ⓒ	ⓓ
3.	ⓐ	ⓑ	ⓒ	ⓓ	8.	ⓐ	ⓑ	ⓒ	ⓓ	13.	ⓐ	ⓑ	ⓒ	ⓓ
4.	ⓐ	ⓑ	ⓒ	ⓓ	9.	ⓐ	ⓑ	ⓒ	ⓓ	14.	ⓐ	ⓑ	ⓒ	ⓓ
5.	ⓐ	ⓑ	ⓒ	ⓓ	10.	ⓐ	ⓑ	ⓒ	ⓓ	15.	ⓐ	ⓑ	ⓒ	ⓓ

▶ Part 4: Mathematics Knowledge

1.	ⓐ	ⓑ	ⓒ	ⓓ	13.	ⓐ	ⓑ	ⓒ	ⓓ	25.	ⓐ	ⓑ	ⓒ	ⓓ
2.	ⓐ	ⓑ	ⓒ	ⓓ	14.	ⓐ	ⓑ	ⓒ	ⓓ	26.	ⓐ	ⓑ	ⓒ	ⓓ
3.	ⓐ	ⓑ	ⓒ	ⓓ	15.	ⓐ	ⓑ	ⓒ	ⓓ	27.	ⓐ	ⓑ	ⓒ	ⓓ
4.	ⓐ	ⓑ	ⓒ	ⓓ	16.	ⓐ	ⓑ	ⓒ	ⓓ	28.	ⓐ	ⓑ	ⓒ	ⓓ
5.	ⓐ	ⓑ	ⓒ	ⓓ	17.	ⓐ	ⓑ	ⓒ	ⓓ	29.	ⓐ	ⓑ	ⓒ	ⓓ
6.	ⓐ	ⓑ	ⓒ	ⓓ	18.	ⓐ	ⓑ	ⓒ	ⓓ	30.	ⓐ	ⓑ	ⓒ	ⓓ
7.	ⓐ	ⓑ	ⓒ	ⓓ	19.	ⓐ	ⓑ	ⓒ	ⓓ	31.	ⓐ	ⓑ	ⓒ	ⓓ
8.	ⓐ	ⓑ	ⓒ	ⓓ	20.	ⓐ	ⓑ	ⓒ	ⓓ	32.	ⓐ	ⓑ	ⓒ	ⓓ
9.	ⓐ	ⓑ	ⓒ	ⓓ	21.	ⓐ	ⓑ	ⓒ	ⓓ	33.	ⓐ	ⓑ	ⓒ	ⓓ
10.	ⓐ	ⓑ	ⓒ	ⓓ	22.	ⓐ	ⓑ	ⓒ	ⓓ	34.	ⓐ	ⓑ	ⓒ	ⓓ
11.	ⓐ	ⓑ	ⓒ	ⓓ	23.	ⓐ	ⓑ	ⓒ	ⓓ	35.	ⓐ	ⓑ	ⓒ	ⓓ
12.	ⓐ	ⓑ	ⓒ	ⓓ	24.	ⓐ	ⓑ	ⓒ	ⓓ					

► Part 1: Arithmetic Reasoning

Time: 36 minutes

1. Mr. Anthony Blake has inherited some musical instruments from his father. They are:

1 violin valued at	$3,500
2 violin bows, each valued at	$850
2 music stands, each valued at	$85
1 cello valued at	$2,300

    In addition, Mr. Blake's father has left him a watch, valued at $250, and some old sheet music valued at $85 total. What is the value of Mr. Blake's inheritance?
    a. $6,735
    b. $7,070
    c. $7,670
    d. $8,005

2. On the cardiac ward, there are 7 nursing assistants. NA Basil has 8 patients; NA Hobbes has 5 patients; NA McGuire has 9 patients; NA Hicks has 10 patients; NA Garcia has 10 patients; NA James has 14 patients, and NA Davis has 7 patients. What is the average number of patients per nursing assistant?
    a. 7
    b. 8
    c. 9
    d. 10

3. If a particular woman's resting heartbeat is 72 beats per minute and she is at rest for $6\frac{1}{2}$ hours, about how many times will her heart beat during that period of time?
    a. 4,320
    b. 28,080
    c. 4,680
    d. 43,200

4. A patient's hospice stay cost $\frac{1}{4}$ as much as his visit to the emergency room. His home nursing cost twice as much as his hospice stay. If his total healthcare bill was $140,000, how much did his home nursing cost?
    a. $10,000
    b. $20,000
    c. $40,000
    d. $80,000

5. Chuck is making a patio using $1\frac{1}{2}$ foot cement squares. The patio will be 10 cement squares by 10 cement squares. If the cement squares are placed right next to each other without any space in between, what will the dimensions of the patio be?
    a. 10 ft by 10 ft
    b. 20 ft by 20 ft
    c. $12\frac{1}{2}$ ft by $12\frac{1}{2}$ ft
    d. 15 ft by 15 ft

6. At a certain school, half the students are female and one-twelfth of the students are from outside the state. What proportion of the students would you expect to be females from outside the state?
    a. $\frac{1}{12}$
    b. $\frac{1}{24}$
    c. $\frac{1}{6}$
    d. $\frac{1}{3}$

7. Which of the following has a 9 in the thousandths place?
    a. 3.0095
    b. 3.0905
    c. 3.9005
    d. 3.0059

8. Based on the information below, estimate the weight of a person who is 5′5″ tall.

HEIGHT	WEIGHT
5′	110 pounds
6′	170 pounds

   a. 125
   b. 130
   c. 135
   d. 140

9. During exercise, a person's heart rate should be between 60% and 90% of the difference between 220 and the person's age. According to this guideline, what should a 30-year-old person's maximum heart rate be during exercise?
   a. 114
   b. 132
   c. 171
   d. 198

10. The local firefighters are doing a "fill the boot" fundraiser. Their goal is to raise $3,500. After three hours, they have raised $2,275. Which statement below is accurate?
   a. They have raised 35% of their goal.
   b. They have $\frac{7}{20}$ of their goal left to raise.
   c. They have raised less than $\frac{1}{2}$ of their goal.
   d. They have raised more than $\frac{3}{4}$ of their goal.

11. A certain water pollutant is unsafe at a level of 20 ppm (parts per million). A city's water supply now contains 50 ppm of this pollutant. What percentage improvement will make the water safe?
   a. 30%
   b. 40%
   c. 50%
   d. 60%

12. In half of migraine sufferers, a certain drug reduces the number of migraines by 50%. What percentage of all migraines can be eliminated by this drug?
   a. 25%
   b. 50%
   c. 75%
   d. 100%

13. Joey, Aaron, Barbara, and Stu have been collecting pennies and putting them in identical containers. Joey's container is $\frac{3}{4}$ full, Aaron's is $\frac{3}{5}$ full, Barbara's is $\frac{2}{3}$ full, and Stu's is $\frac{2}{5}$ full. Whose container has the most pennies?
   a. Joey
   b. Aaron
   c. Barbara
   d. Stu

14. Rosa kept track of how many hours she spent reading during the month of August. The first week she read for $4\frac{1}{2}$ hours, the second week for $3\frac{3}{4}$ hours, the third week for $8\frac{1}{2}$ hours, and the fourth week for $1\frac{1}{3}$ hours. How many hours altogether did she spend reading in the month of August?
   a. $17\frac{47}{60}$
   b. 16
   c. $16\frac{1}{8}$
   d. $18\frac{2}{15}$

15. A study shows that 600,000 women die each year in pregnancy and childbirth, one-fifth more than scientists previously estimated. How many such deaths did the scientists previously estimate?
   a. 120,000
   b. 300,000
   c. 480,000
   d. 500,000

16. A gram of fat contains nine calories. An 1,800-calorie diet allows no more than 20% calories from fat. How many grams of fat are allowed in that diet?
 a. 40 g
 b. 90 g
 c. 200 g
 d. 360 g

17. What is 250 mg in terms of grams?
 a. 0.0250 g
 b. 0.250 g
 c. 2.50 g
 d. 250,000 g

18. After three days, a group of hikers discovers that they have used $\frac{2}{5}$ of their supplies. At this rate, how many more days can they go forward before they have to turn around?
 a. 0.75 days
 b. 3.75 days
 c. 4.5 days
 d. 7.5 days

19. A supply truck can carry three tons. A breakfast ration weighs 12 ounces, and the other two daily meals weigh 18 ounces each. On a ten-day trip, how many troops can be supplied by one truck?
 a. 100
 b. 150
 c. 200
 d. 320

20. A clerk can process 26 forms per hour. If 5,600 forms must be processed in an eight-hour day, how many clerks must you hire for that day?
 a. 24 clerks
 b. 25 clerks
 c. 26 clerks
 d. 27 clerks

21. On the same latitude, Company E travels east at 35 miles per hour and Company F travels west at 15 miles per hour. If the two companies start out 2,100 miles apart, how long will it take them to meet?
 a. 42 hours
 b. 60 hours
 c. 105 hours
 d. 140 hours

22. During the last week of training on an obstacle course, a recruit achieves the following times in seconds: 66, 57, 54, 54, 64, 59, and 59. The recruit's three best times this week are averaged for his final score on the course. What is his final score?
 a. 57 seconds
 b. 55 seconds
 c. 59 seconds
 d. 61 seconds

23. Mike types three times as fast as Nick. Together they type 24 pages per hour. If Nick learns to type as fast as Mike, how much will they be able to type per hour?
 a. 30 pages
 b. 36 pages
 c. 40 pages
 d. 48 pages

24. If you take recyclables to whichever recycler will pay the most, what is the greatest amount of money you could get for 2,200 pounds of aluminum, 1,400 pounds of cardboard, 3,100 pounds of glass, and 900 pounds of plastic?

	ALUM-INUM	CARD-BOARD	GLASS	PLASTIC
Recycler X	6 cents/pound	3 cents/pound	8 cents/pound	2 cents/pound
Recycler Y	7 cents/pound	4 cents/pound	7 cents/pound	3 cents/pound

    a. $440
    b. $447
    c. $454
    d. $485

25. Water is coming into a tank three times as fast as it is going out. After one hour, the tank contains 11,400 gallons of water. How fast is the water coming in?

    a. $\frac{3,800 \text{ gallons}}{\text{hour}}$
    b. $\frac{5,700 \text{ gallons}}{\text{hour}}$
    c. $\frac{11,400 \text{ gallons}}{\text{hour}}$
    d. $\frac{17,100 \text{ gallons}}{\text{hour}}$

26. A train must travel 3,450 miles in six days. How many miles must it travel each day?
    a. 525
    b. 550
    c. 600
    d. 575

27. A uniform requires four square yards of cloth. To produce uniforms for 84,720 troops, how much cloth is required?
    a. 330,880 square yards
    b. 336,880 square yards
    c. 338,880 square yards
    d. 340,880 square yards

28. A dormitory now houses 30 men and allows 42 square feet of space per man. If five more men are put into this dormitory, how much less space will each man have?
    a. 5 square feet
    b. 6 square feet
    c. 7 square feet
    d. 8 square feet

29. Ron is half as old as Sam, who is three times as old as Ted. The sum of their ages is 55. How old is Ron?
    a. 5
    b. 10
    c. 15
    d. 30

30. To lower a fever of 105°F, ice packs are applied for one minute and then removed for five minutes before being applied again. Each application lowers the fever by half a degree. How long will it take to lower the fever to 99°F?
    a. one hour
    b. one hour and 12 minutes
    c. one hour and 15 minutes
    d. one hour and 30 minutes

▶ Part 2: Word Knowledge

Time: 11 minutes

Select the choice that best matches the underlined word.

1. Erroneous most nearly means
   a. digressive.
   b. confused.
   c. impenetrable.
   d. faulty.

2. Grotesque most nearly means
   a. extreme.
   b. frenzied.
   c. hideous.
   d. typical.

3. The Adamsville Kennel Club's ancient computer system was outmoded.
   a. worthless
   b. unusable
   c. obsolete
   d. unnecessary

4. Garbled most nearly means
   a. lucid.
   b. unintelligible.
   c. devoured.
   d. outrageous.

5. Rigorous most nearly means
   a. demanding.
   b. tolerable.
   c. lenient.
   d. disorderly.

6. Flagrant most nearly means
   a. secret.
   b. worthless.
   c. noble.
   d. glaring.

7. Oration most nearly means
   a. nuisance.
   b. independence.
   c. address.
   d. length.

8. Although the police might be able to help Mr. Chen recover his stolen property, he obstinately refuses to file a complaint.
   a. repeatedly
   b. reluctantly
   c. foolishly
   d. stubbornly

9. The student's glib remarks irritated the teacher.
   a. angry
   b. superficial
   c. insulting
   d. dishonest

10. Composure most nearly means
   a. agitation.
   b. poise.
   c. liveliness.
   d. stimulation.

11. Eccentric most nearly means
   a. normal.
   b. frugal.
   c. peculiar.
   d. selective.

12. <u>Commendable</u> most nearly means
  a. admirable.
  b. accountable.
  c. irresponsible.
  d. noticeable.

13. <u>Oblivious</u> most nearly means
  a. visible.
  b. sinister.
  c. aware.
  d. ignorant.

14. <u>Philanthropy</u> most nearly means
  a. selfishness.
  b. fascination.
  c. disrespect.
  d. generosity.

15. Most members of the conservative community thought the neighbor's bright pink Corvette was <u>ostentatious</u>.
  a. hilarious
  b. pretentious
  c. outrageous
  d. obnoxious

16. <u>Passive</u> most nearly means
  a. resigned.
  b. emotional.
  c. lively.
  d. woeful.

17. <u>Proximity</u> most nearly means
  a. distance.
  b. agreement.
  c. nearness.
  d. intelligence.

18. <u>Negligible</u> most nearly means
  a. insignificant.
  b. delicate.
  c. meaningful.
  d. illegible.

19. <u>Rational</u> most nearly means
  a. deliberate.
  b. invalid.
  c. prompt.
  d. sound.

20. <u>Vigilant</u> most nearly means
  a. nonchalant.
  b. alert.
  c. righteous.
  d. strenuous.

21. <u>Astute</u> most nearly means
  a. perceptive.
  b. inattentive.
  c. stubborn.
  d. elegant.

22. The <u>prerequisite</u> training to belong to this team is a three-hour course in volleyball.
  a. required
  b. optional
  c. preferred
  d. advisable

23. <u>Coerce</u> most nearly means
  a. permit.
  b. waste.
  c. compel.
  d. deny.

24. Collaborate most nearly means
  a. cooperate.
  b. coordinate.
  c. entice.
  d. elaborate.

25. Abrupt most nearly means
  a. interrupt.
  b. brusque.
  c. extended.
  d. corrupt.

▶ Part 3: Paragraph Comprehension

Time: 13 minutes

Read each passage and answer the questions that follow.

Police officers must read suspects their Miranda rights upon taking them into custody. When a suspect who is merely being questioned incriminates himself, he might later seek to have the case dismissed on the grounds of not having been apprised of his Miranda rights when arrested. Therefore, officers must take care not to give suspects grounds for later claiming they believed themselves to be in custody.

1. What is the main idea of the passage?
  a. Officers must remember to read suspects their Miranda rights.
  b. Suspects sometimes mistakenly believe they are in custody when in fact they are only being questioned.
  c. Officers who are merely questioning a suspect must not give the suspect the impression that he or she is in custody.
  d. Miranda rights needn't be read to all suspects before questioning.

2. When must police officers read Miranda rights to a suspect?
  a. while questioning the suspect
  b. while placing the suspect under arrest
  c. before taking the suspect to the police station
  d. before releasing the suspect

Dilly's Deli provides a dining experience like no other! Recently relocated to the old market area, Dilly's is especially popular for lunch. At the counter, you can place your order for one of Dilly's three daily lunch specials or one of several sandwiches, all at reasonable prices. Once you get your food, choose a seat at one of the four charming communal tables. By the time you are ready to carry your paper plate to the trash bin, you have experienced some of the best food and most charming company our city has to offer.

3. According to the passage, if you eat lunch at Dilly's Deli, you should expect to
  a. be surrounded by antiques.
  b. place your order with the waiter who comes to your table.
  c. carry your own food to your table.
  d. be asked out on a date by someone charming.

4. The main purpose of the passage is to
  a. profile the owner of Dilly's Deli.
  b. describe the kind of food served at Dilly's Deli.
  c. encourage people to eat at Dilly's Deli.
  d. explain the historical significance of the Dilly's Deli Building.

There are two types of diabetes, insulin-dependent and non-insulin-dependent. Between 90 and 95% of the estimated 13 to 14 million people in the United States with diabetes have non-insulin-dependent, or Type II, diabetes. Its symptoms often develop gradually and are hard to identify at first; therefore, nearly half of all people with diabetes do not know they have it. This can be particularly dangerous because untreated diabetes can cause damage to the heart, blood vessels, eyes, kidneys, and nerves. While the causes, short-term effects, and treatments of Type I and Type II diabetes differ, both types can cause the same long-term health problems.

5. According to the passage, which of the following may be the most dangerous aspect of Type II diabetes?
   a. Insulin shots are needed daily for treatment of Type II diabetes.
   b. In Type II diabetes the pancreas does not produce insulin.
   c. Type II diabetes interferes with digestion.
   d. Persons with Type II diabetes may not know they have it and will therefore not seek treatment.

6. Which of the following are the same for Type I and Type II diabetes?
   a. treatments
   b. long-term health risks
   c. short-term effects
   d. causes

Because crimes against adolescents are likely to be committed by offenders of the same age (as well as same sex and race), preventing violence among and against adolescents is a two-fold challenge. New violence-prevention programs in urban middle schools help reduce the crime rate by teaching both victims and perpetrators the skills of conflict resolution and how to apply reason to disputes, as well

as by changing attitudes towards achieving respect through violence and towards the need to retaliate.

7. What is the main idea of the passage?
   a. Middle school violence-prevention programs are designed to help to lower the rate of crimes against adolescents.
   b. Adolescents are more likely to commit crimes than older people and must therefore be taught nonviolence in order to protect society.
   c. Middle school students appreciate the conflict resolution skills they acquire in violence-prevention programs.
   d. Violence against adolescents is increasing.

8. According to the passage, why is preventing violence against adolescents a *two-fold challenge*?
   a. because adolescents are as likely to be victims of violent crime as members of other age groups
   b. because adolescents must be prevented from both perpetrating and being victimized by violent crime
   c. because adolescents must change both their violent behavior and their attitudes towards violence
   d. because adolescents are vulnerable, yet reluctant to listen to adult advice

Beginning next month, the department will institute a program intended to remove the graffiti from trucks. Any truck that finishes its assigned route before the end of the workers' shift will return to the lot where supervisors will provide materials for workers to use in cleaning the trucks. Because the length of time it takes to complete different routes varies, trucks will no longer be assigned to a specific route but will be rotated among the routes. Therefore, workers should no longer leave personal items in the trucks, as they will not necessarily be driving the same truck each day as in the past.

9. According to the passage, the removal of graffiti from trucks will be done by
a. supervisors.
b. workers.
c. janitorial staff.
d. prisoners doing community service.

10. According to the passage, routes
a. vary in the amount of time they take to complete.
b. all take seven hours to complete.
c. are all of equal length.
d. take longer to complete at certain times of the year.

11. According to the passage, prior to the graffiti clean-up program, workers
a. were not responsible for cleaning the trucks.
b. had to repaint the trucks every month.
c. usually drove the same truck each workday.
d. were not allowed to leave personal belongings in the trucks.

Some people argue that retribution is the purpose of punishing a person convicted of a crime, and that therefore the punishment must in some direct way fit the crime. Another view, the deterrence theory, promotes punishment in order to discourage commission of future crimes. In this view, punishment need not relate directly to the crime committed. However, punishment must necessarily be uniform and consistently applied, in order for the members of the public to understand how they would be punished if they committed a crime.

12. The passage suggests that a person who believes that the death penalty results in fewer murders most likely also believes in
a. the deterrence theory.
b. the retribution theory.
c. giving judges considerable discretion in imposing sentences.
d. the integrity of the criminal justice system.

13. A person who believes in the deterrence theory would probably also support
a. non-unanimous jury verdicts.
b. early release of prisoners because of prison overcrowding.
c. a broad definition of the insanity defense.
d. allowing television broadcasts of court proceedings.

The city ordinance reads, "Sanitation workers will not collect garbage in containers weighing more than fifty pounds." Workers are expected to use their best judgment in determining when a container weighs more than fifty pounds. If a container is too heavy, workers should attach one of the pre-printed warning messages (which are carried in all trucks) to the container, informing the household that the container weighs more than fifty pounds and cannot be collected.

14. According to the passage, in order to determine if a container is too heavy, sanitation workers should
a. carry a scale in their truck to weigh containers.
b. practice lifting fifty pounds at home to know what it feels like.
c. assume any container he or she can lift weighs less than fifty pounds.
d. use her or his best guess whether a container weighs more than fifty pounds.

15. According to the passage, if a sanitation worker believes that a container weighs more than fifty pounds, he or she should
   a. attach a pre-printed warning to the container and leave it where it is.
   b. write a note to the household, informing them of the weight limit.
   c. collect it anyway, as the household probably did not know about the weight limit.
   d. notify a special collections truck.

► Part 4: Mathematics Knowledge

Time: 24 minutes

1. $-\frac{5}{3} - \frac{1}{3} =$
   a. $\frac{4}{3}$
   b. $-\frac{4}{3}$
   c. 2
   d. −2

2. The area of a region is measured in
   a. units.
   b. square units.
   c. cubic units.
   d. quadrants.

3. When calculating the area of a figure, you are finding
   a. the distance around the object.
   b. the length of a side.
   c. the amount of space that the object covers.
   d. the number of sides it has.

4. $(25 + 17)(64 - 49) =$
   a. 57
   b. 630
   c. 570
   d. 63

5. $12(84 - 5) - (3 \times 54) =$
   a. 54,000
   b. 841
   c. 796
   d. 786

6. Which of the following numbers is the smallest?
   a. $\frac{6}{10}$
   b. $\frac{8}{15}$
   c. $\frac{33}{60}$
   d. $\frac{11}{20}$

7. Which of the following is the equivalent of $\frac{13}{25}$?
   a. 0.38
   b. 0.4
   c. 0.48
   d. 0.52

8. What is another way to write 0.32×10^3?
   a. 3.2
   b. 32
   c. 320
   d. 3,200

9. How does the area of a rectangle change if both the base and the height of the original rectangle are tripled?
   a. The area is tripled.
   b. The area is six times larger.
   c. The area is nine times larger.
   d. The area remains the same.

10. When measuring the area of a football field, you would most likely use
   a. square inches.
   b. square millimeters.
   c. square miles.
   d. square yards.

11. On the number line below, point L is to be located halfway between points M and N. What number will correspond to point L?

a. $-\frac{1}{4}$

b. $-\frac{1}{2}$

c. $-1\frac{1}{4}$

d. 0

12. Which of the following statements is true?

a. Parallel lines intersect at right angles.

b. Parallel lines never intersect.

c. Perpendicular lines never intersect.

d. Intersecting lines have two points in common.

13. What is another way to write 2.75×100^2?

a. 275

b. 2,750

c. 27,500

d. 275,000

14. $(a^2b)^2(2ab)^3$ is equivalent to which of the following?

a. $2a^3b^5$

b. $5ab$

c. $6a^7b$

d. $8a^7b$

15. What is the next number in the series below?

3 16 6 12 12 8 _____

a. 4

b. 15

c. 20

d. 24

16. Which number sentence is true?

a. $4.3 < 0.43$

b. $0.43 < 0.043$

c. $0.043 > 0.0043$

d. $0.0043 > 0.043$

17. If $x = 6$, $y = -2$, and $z = 3$, what is the value of the following expression?

$$xz - \frac{-xy}{z^2}$$

a. $-\frac{2}{3}$

b. $\frac{2}{3}$

c. $3\frac{1}{3}$

d. 5

18. What is the area of a triangle with a height of 10 inches and a base of 2 inches?

a. 10 square inches

b. 12 square inches

c. 20 square inches

d. 22 square inches

19. What is 0.716 rounded to the nearest tenth?

a. 0.7

b. 0.8

c. 0.72

d. 1.0

20. If $\frac{x}{2} + \frac{x}{6} = 4$, what is x?

a. $\frac{1}{24}$

b. $\frac{1}{6}$

c. 3

d. 6

21. Choose the answer to the following problem:

$10^5 \div 10^2 =$

a. 10

b. 10^3

c. 10^7

d. 10^{10}

22. If a population of cells grows from 10 to 320 in a period of five hours, what is the rate of growth?

a. It doubles its numbers every half hour.

b. It doubles its numbers every hour.

c. It triples its numbers every hour.

d. It doubles its numbers every two hours.

23. $3.16 \div 0.079 =$

a. 0.025

b. 2.5

c. 4.0

d. 40

24. $2\frac{5}{8} \div \frac{1}{3} =$

a. $7\frac{7}{8}$

b. $8\frac{1}{3}$

c. $5\frac{11}{24}$

d. $\frac{7}{8}$

25. $\frac{11}{5}$ is equal to

a. 2.25.

b. 1.5.

c. 1.15.

d. 2.20.

26. What is the area of the figure below?

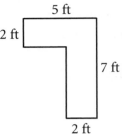

a. 19 square feet

b. 20 square feet

c. 24 square feet

d. 38 square feet

27. What is $7\frac{1}{5}\%$ of 465, rounded to the nearest tenth?

a. 32.5

b. 33

c. 33.5

d. 34

28. What kind of polygon is the figure below?

a. heptagon

b. octagon

c. hexagon

d. pentagon

29. Which of the following is equivalent to $2y^2$?

a. $2(y + y)$

b. $2y(y)$

c. $y^2 + 2$

d. $y + y + y + y$

30. For which of the following values of *x* is this number sentence true: $25 - x < 10$?

    a. 16

    b. 15

    c. 14

    d. 13

31. How much water must be added to one liter of a 5% saline solution to get a 2% saline solution?

    a. 1 L

    b. 2 L

    c. 1.5 L

    d. 2.5 L

32. What is the decimal form of $\frac{5}{6}$? (Round two decimal places.)

    a. 0.65

    b. 0.88

    c. 0.83

    d. 0.13

33. $15 \text{ cc} \times 1.2 =$

    a. 17 cc

    b. 18 cc

    c. 30 cc

    d. 35 cc

34. What is the volume of liquid that is remaining in this cylinder?

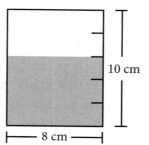

10 cm

8 cm

    a. $64\pi \text{ cm}^3$

    b. $80\pi \text{ cm}^3$

    c. $96\pi \text{ cm}^3$

    d. $160\pi \text{ cm}^3$

35. $-0.05 =$

    a. $\frac{1}{20}$

    b. $-\frac{1}{20}$

    c. $\frac{1}{2}$

    d. $-\frac{1}{2}$

▶ Answers

Part 1: Arithmetic Reasoning

1. d. Don't forget that there are two bows and two music stands, and remember to add the value of the watch and the sheet music.

2. c. First, add the number of patients to find the total: 63. Then divide the number of patients by the number of nursing assistants: 63 divided by 7 is 9.

3. b. This is a two-step multiplication problem. To find out how many heartbeats there would be in one hour, you must multiply 72 by 60 (minutes) and then multiply this result, 4,320, by 6.5 hours.

4. c. Let E = emergency room cost; H = hospice cost, which is $(\frac{1}{4})E$; N = home nursing cost, which is $2E$, or $2(\frac{1}{4})E$. The total bill is $E + H + N$, which is $E + (\frac{1}{4})E + (\frac{2}{4})E$, = 140,000. Add the left side of the equation to get $\frac{7}{4}E$ = 140,000. To solve for E, multiply both sides of the equation by $(\frac{4}{7})$; $E = 140,000(\frac{4}{7})$, or 80,000; $H = (\frac{1}{4})E$, or 20,000, and $N = 2H$, or 40,000.

5. d. Multiply $1\frac{1}{2}$ by 10. Change $1\frac{1}{2}$ to an improper fraction $(\frac{3}{2})$ and make 10 into a fraction by placing it over 1 $(\frac{10}{1})$; $\frac{3}{2} \times \frac{10}{1} = \frac{30}{2}$ = 15 feet. Each side is 15 feet long, so the dimensions are 15 ft by 15 ft.

6. b. If half the students are female, then you would expect half of the out-of-state students to be female. One half of $\frac{1}{12}$ is $\frac{1}{24}$.

7. a. In choice **b**, the 9 is in the hundredths place; in choice **c**, it is in the tenths place; and in choice **d**, it is in the ten thousandths place.

8. c. A foot in height makes a difference of 60 pounds, or 5 pounds per inch of height over 5′. A person who is 5′5″ is (5)(5 pounds), or 25 pounds, heavier than the person who is 5′, so add 25 pounds to 110 pounds to get 135 pounds.

9. c. The difference between 220 and this person's age is 190. The maximum heart rate is 90% of this: $(0.9)(190) = 171$.

10. a. The part of their goal that they have raised is $2,275 and the whole goal is $3,500. The fraction for this is $\frac{2,275}{3,500}$. The numerator and denominator can both be divided by 175 to get a simplified fraction of $\frac{13}{20}$. They have completed $\frac{13}{20}$ of their goal, which means that they have $\frac{7}{20}$ left to go $(\frac{20}{20} - \frac{13}{20} = \frac{7}{20})$.

11. d. Thirty ppm of the pollutant would have to be removed to bring the 50 ppm down to 20 ppm. Thirty ppm represents 60% of 50 ppm.

12. a. The drug is 50% effective for 50% of migraine sufferers, so it eliminates $(0.50) \times (0.50)$, or 0.25 of all migraines.

13. a. Compare $\frac{3}{4}, \frac{3}{5}, \frac{2}{3}, \frac{2}{5}$ by finding a common denominator. The common denominator for 3, 4, and 5 is 60. Multiply the numerator and denominator of a fraction by the same number so that the denominator becomes 60. The fractions then become $\frac{45}{60}, \frac{36}{60}, \frac{40}{60},$ and $\frac{24}{60}$. The fraction with the largest numerator is the largest fraction; $\frac{45}{60}$ is the largest fraction. It is equivalent to Joey's fraction of $\frac{3}{4}$.

14. a. Add the number of hours together using a common denominator of 60; $4\frac{30}{60} + 3\frac{45}{60} + 8\frac{12}{60} = 1\frac{20}{60} = 16\frac{107}{60}$, which is simplified to $17\frac{47}{60}$ hours.

15. d. Let E = the estimate. *One-fifth more than the estimate* means $\frac{6}{5}$ or 120% of E, so $600,000 = (1.20)(E)$. Dividing both sides by 1.2 leaves $E = 500,000$.

16. a. 20% of 1,800, or $(0.2)(1,800) = 360$ calories are allowed from fat. Since there are nine calories in each gram of fat, divide 360 by 9 to find that 40 grams of fat are allowed.

17. b. 250 milligrams is $\frac{250}{1,000}$ gram, or 0.250 g.

18. **a.** First find out how long the entire hike can be, based on the rate at which the hikers are using their supplies. If 1 = all supplies and x = entire hike, then $\frac{\frac{2}{5}}{3} = \frac{1}{x}$. Cross multiply to get $\frac{2x}{5} = 3$, so that $x = \frac{(3)(5)}{2}$, or $7\frac{1}{2}$ days for the length of the entire hike. This means that the hikers could go forward for 3.75 days altogether before they would have to turn around. They have already hiked for three days, which leaves 0.75 for the amount of time they can now go forward before having to turn around.

19. **c.** Three tons is 6,000 pounds; 6,000 pounds multiplied by 16 ounces per pound is 96,000 ounces. The total weight of each daily ration is 48 ounces. Ninety-six thousand divided by 48 is 2,000 troops supplied. Two thousand divided by 10 days is 200 troops supplied.

20. **d.** Twenty-six forms multiplied by 8 hours is 208 forms per day per clerk. Fifty-six hundred divided by 208 is approximately 26.9, which means you have to hire 27 clerks for the day.

21. **a.** The companies' combined rate of travel is 50 miles per hour. 2,100 miles divided by 50 miles per hour is 42 hours.

22. **b.** The recruit's three best times are 54, 54, and 57. To find the average, add the 3 numbers and divide the sum by 3.

23. **b.** $M = 3N$; $3N + N = 24$, so that $N = 6$. Since $M = 3N$, $M = 18$. If Nick catches up to Mike's typing speed, then both M and N will equal 18, and then the combined rate will be 36 pages per hour.

24. **d.** $2,200(0.07) = \$154$; $\$154 + 1,400(0.04) = \$210$; $\$210 + 3,100(0.08) = \$458$; $\$458 + \$900(0.03) = \$485$.

25. **d.** $3w$ = water coming in; w = water going out; $3w - w = 11,400$, which means that w is 5,700 and $3w$ is 17,100.

26. **d.** 3,450 miles divided by 6 days is 575 miles.

27. **c.** 84,720 troops multiplied by 4 square yards of cloth is 338,880 square yards of cloth required.

28. **b.** 30 men multiplied by 42 square feet of space is 1,260 square feet of space; 1,260 square feet divided by 35 men is 36 square feet, so each man will have 6 less square feet of space.

29. **c.** Let T = Ted's age; S = Sam's age = $3T$; R = Ron's age = $\frac{S}{2}$, or $\frac{3T}{2}$. The sum of the ages is 55, which means $T + 3T + \frac{3T}{2} = 55$. Find the common denominator (2) to add the left side of the equation; $T = 10$. If Ted is 10, then Sam is 30, and Ron is $\frac{3T}{2}$, which is 15 years old.

30. **b.** The difference between 105 and 99 is 6 degrees. The temperature is lowered by half a degree every six minutes, or 1 degree every 12 minutes; 6 degrees multiplied by 12 minutes per degree is 72 minutes, or 1 hour and 12 minutes.

Part 2: Word Knowledge

1. **d.** Something that is *erroneous* is wrong or *faulty*.

2. **c.** Something that is *grotesque* is distorted, misshapen, or *hideous*.

3. **c.** To be *outmoded* is to be out-of-date or *obsolete*.

4. **b.** A statement that is *garbled* is scrambled and confusing, or *unintelligible*.

5. **a.** Something that is *rigorous* is strict or *demanding*.

6. **d.** A thing that is *flagrant* is conspicuous or *glaring*.

7. **c.** An *oration* is a formal speech or an *address*.

8. **d.** When something is done *obstinately,* it is done in a refractory manner or *stubbornly*.

9. **b.** A *glib* remark is a quick and insincere, or *superficial,* one.

10. **b.** When someone has *composure,* that person has self-possession or *poise*.

11. **c.** To be *eccentric* is to be unconventional or *peculiar.*

12. **a.** If something is *commendable* it is praiseworthy or *admirable.*

13. **d.** To be *oblivious* of something is to be unaware or *ignorant* of it.

14. **d.** An act of *philanthropy* is an act of charity or *generosity.*

15. **b.** To be *ostentatious* is to be showy or *pretentious.*

16. **a.** To be *passive* is to be compliant and accepting, or *resigned.*

17. **c.** When something is in *proximity* to something else, it is close or in *nearness* to it.

18. **a.** To be *negligible* is to be unimportant or *insignificant.*

19. **d.** A *rational* judgment is a logical or *sound* one.

20. **b.** To be *vigilant* is to be watchful or *alert.*

21. **a.** To be *astute* is to be keen-minded or *perceptive.*

22. **a.** A *prerequisite* is something that is necessary or *required.*

23. **c.** To *coerce* someone to do something is to force, pressure, or *compel* that person to do it.

24. **a.** To *collaborate* on a project is to work together or *cooperate* on it.

25. **b.** To be *abrupt* is to be curt or *brusque.*

Part 3: Paragraph Comprehension

1. **a.** While choices **b** and **c** are true, they are not the main idea. Choice **d** is contradicted in the last sentence.

2. **b.** See the first sentence of the passage.

3. **c.** This is the only one of the choices that is stated in the passage (in the third and fourth sentences). Choices **a** and **d** are not stated in the passage. Choice **b** is contradicted by the passage.

4. **c.** The whole tone of the passage is complimentary to Dilly's. Choices **a** and **d** are not mentioned in the passage. Although choice **b** is mentioned, it is not the main point.

5. **d.** The passage mentions that the symptoms of Type II diabetes may occur gradually and thus be attributed to other causes. Left untreated, diabetes can cause damage to several major organs in the body.

6. **b.** According to the passage, only the long-term health problems are the same for these two different disorders.

7. **a.** None of the other choices is mentioned in the passage.

8. **b.** This idea is explicitly stated in the first sentence.

9. **b.** See the second sentence of the passage.

10. **a.** See the third sentence of the passage.

11. **c.** The last sentence of the passage implies that, in the past, sanitation workers usually drove the same truck each day.

12. **a.** This can be deduced from the second sentence of the passage.

13. **d.** The last sentence notes that the deterrence theory has the effect of teaching not only criminals, but also the public.

14. **d.** Although the other options are not precluded by the passage, the passage only requires workers to make an educated guess as to the weight of the container.

15. **a.** See the third sentence of the passage.

Part 4: Mathematics Knowledge

1. **d.** Subtract to get $-\frac{6}{3}$, which reduces to -2.

2. **b.** When calculating area, you are finding the number of square units that cover the region.

3. **c.** The area of a figure is the amount of space the object covers, in square units.

4. **b.** Perform the operations within the parentheses first, which gives you $(42)(15) = 630$.

5. d. Perform the operations in the parentheses first: $(12)(79) - 162 = 786$.

6. b. Fractions must be converted to the lowest common denominator, which allows you to compare the amounts: $\frac{36}{60}, \frac{32}{60}, \frac{33}{60},$ and $\frac{33}{60}$.

7. d. The fraction $\frac{13}{25}$ is equal to $\frac{52}{100}$.

8. c. $(0.32)(10^3) = 0.32 \times (10 \times 10 \times 10)$.

9. c. Since both dimensions are tripled, there are two additional factors of 3. Therefore, the new area is $3 \times 3 = 9$ times as large as the original.

10. d. A football field would most likely be measured in square yards. Square inches and square millimeters are too small, and square miles are too large.

11. a. The halfway point on the number line is between 0 and $-\frac{1}{2}$, which is $-\frac{1}{4}$.

12. b. Corresponding points on parallel lines are always the same distance apart, so the lines can never intersect.

13. c. $100^2 = (100)(100)$, or 10,000; $(10,000) \times (2.75) = 27,500$.

14. d. Multiply the powers of each set of parentheses to get $a^4b^2(8a^3b^{12})$. When multiplying the outside of the parentheses by the inside, add the exponents.

15. d. This series actually has two alternating sets of numbers. The first number is doubled, giving the third number. The second number has 4 subtracted from it, giving the fourth number. Therefore, the blank space will be 12 doubled, or 24.

16. c. The farther to the right the digits go, the smaller the number.

17. c. Beginning with the operations in the brackets, $[6(3)] - [6(-2)]$ divided by 9 becomes $18 - (-12)$ divided by 9; 30 divided by $9 = \frac{10}{3}$, which is $3\frac{1}{3}$.

18. a. The formula for the area of a triangle is $A = \frac{1}{2}bh; \frac{1}{2}(10)(2) = 10$.

19. a. Choice **c** is rounded to the thousandths place. Choice **d** is rounded to the nearest whole number. Choice **b** is rounded up rather than down.

20. d. To add the left side of the equation, find the common denominator, so that $\frac{3x}{6} + \frac{x}{6} = 4$; $\frac{4x}{6} = 4$; and $4x = 24$.

21. b. In a division problem like this, leave the whole number the same and subtract the exponents.

22. b. You can use trial and error to arrive at a solution to this problem. After the first hour, the number would be 20, after the second hour 40, after the third hour 80, after the fourth hour 160, and after the fifth hour 320. The other answer choices do not have the same outcome.

23. d. Create a division problem without decimals by moving the decimal point three places to the right: 3,160 divided by 79 is 40.

24. a. Convert the mixed number to a fraction: $\frac{21}{8}$ divided by $\frac{1}{3}$ is $(\frac{21}{8})(\frac{3}{1}) = \frac{63}{8}$, or $7\frac{7}{8}$.

25. d. $\frac{11}{5}$ is an improper fraction. One way of solving this problem is to convert the improper fraction into a mixed number that can then be converted into a decimal. A quicker way is to divide the numerator by the denominator, paying close attention to the decimal point; $11 \div 5 = 2.20$.

26. b. Find the area of two rectangles and then add the results. Use an imaginary line to block off the first rectangle at the top of the figure. This rectangle measures $(5 \text{ feet})(2 \text{ feet}) = 10$ square feet. The second rectangle is also $(5 \text{ feet})(2 \text{ feet})$. Add the two together for a total of 20 square feet.

27. c. First, change the percent to a decimal: $(.072) \times (465) = 33.48$, which rounded to the nearest tenth is 33.5.

28. a. A heptagon has seven sides.

29. b. The expression y^2 means y times y.

30. a. $25 - 16 = 9$, which is the only choice that leaves you with a number less than 10.

31. c. Use the equation $(0.05)(1) = (0.02)\,x$: The left side represents 5% of 1 liter; the right side represents 2% of some amount of water. From the equation, $x = 2.5$. Subtracting the 1 liter of water already present in the 5% solution, you will find that 1.5 liters need to be added.

32. c. Divide 5 by 6 to convert the fraction into a decimal; $5 \div 6 = 0.83\overline{33}$. Round two decimal places to get 0.83.

33. b. $(1.20)(15) = 18$ cc.

34. c. The volume of a cylinder equals $\pi r^2 h$, where r is the radius of the cylinder and h is the height. The radius is half the diameter, so the radius of this cylinder is 4 cm. The height of the volume is $10 - 4 = 6$ (the height of the whole cylinder minus the height of space in which the liquid has been poured out). So the volume is $\pi(4)^2(6)$, or $\pi(16)(6) = 96\pi$ cm^3.

35. b. First convert -0.05 into a fraction; $\frac{5 \div 5}{100 \div 5} = \frac{1}{20}$. Then, do not forget to add the negative sign to get $-\frac{1}{20}$.

Scoring

Write your raw score (the number you got right) for each test in the blanks below. Then turn to Chapter 3 to find out how to convert these raw scores into the scores the armed services use.

1. Arithmetic Reasoning: _____ right out of 30
2. Word Knowledge: _____ right out of 25
3. Paragraph Comprehension: _____ right out of 15
4. Mathematics Knowledge: _____ right out of 35

Here are the steps you should take, depending on your AFQT score on this practice test:

- **If your AFQT is below 29,** you need more help in reading and/or math. You should spend plenty of time reviewing the lessons and practice questions found in this book.

- **If your AFQT is 29–31,** be sure to focus on your weakest subjects in the review lessons and practice questions that are found in this book.

- **If your AFQT is above 31,** review areas that give you trouble, if any. Then, take the official exam with confidence knowing you are well prepared.